T0360758

Financial Communication

This essential guide to financial communication provides a concise critical overview of this increasingly important field. It challenges existing assumptions about the role and significance of financial public relations (PR) and investor relations, and the dominant paradigm of shareholder value. This book explores how the dominant paradigm in financial PR is based on the methodologically and historically incorrect assumption of symmetrical communication.

Highlighting the importance of financial communications in the corporate hierarchy where it is often a direct function of the Finance Director, this book critically assesses its ideological role in normalising the idea and role of 'the market' and promotes the neoliberal view that the sole function of the public company is to increase shareholder value. It opens up new theoretical perspectives by considering retail investor behaviour from the perspective of fandom theory through the behaviour of investors during financial booms, busts and bubbles.

This volume will be of interest to researchers in the fields of PR, financial communication, accounting and financial management as well as practitioners working in financial PR and investor relations.

Keith Butterick is an award-winning former business journalist. As a director of a financial PR consultancy, he worked on all aspects of the public company life, financial calendar work, company flotations and contested takeovers. He lectured on journalism and PR at the University of Huddersfield. He is the author of two books, *Introducing Public Relations: Theory and Practice* by SAGE and *Complacency and Collusion: A Critical Introduction to Finance and Business Journalism*. A consultant on engagement and participation, he advises companies and organisations on effective participation strategies.

Routledge New Directions in PR & Communication Research

Edited by Kevin Moloney

Current academic thinking about public relations (PR) and related communication is a lively, expanding marketplace of ideas and many scholars believe that it's time for its radical approach to be deepened. Routledge New Directions in PR & Communication Research is the forum of choice for this new thinking. Its key strength is its remit, publishing critical and challenging responses to continuities and fractures in contemporary PR thinking and practice, tracking its spread into new geographies and political economies. It questions its contested role in market-orientated, capitalist, liberal democracies around the world, and examines its invasion of all media spaces, old, new, and as yet unenvisaged.

The New Directions series has already published and commissioned diverse original work on topics such as:

- PR's influence on Israeli and Palestinian nation-building
- PR's origins in the history of ideas
- a Jungian approach to PR ethics and professionalism
- global perspectives on PR professional practice
- PR as an everyday language for everyone
- PR as emotional labor
- PR as communication in conflicted societies, and
- PR's relationships to cooperation, justice, and paradox.

We actively invite new contributions and offer academics a welcoming place for the publication of their analyses of a universal, persuasive mindset that lives comfortably in old and new media around the world.

Digital Public Relations and Marketing Communication Trends in Africa
Edited by Anne W. Njathi and Brandi Watkins

Financial Communication
A Critical Assessment
Keith Butterick

For more information about this series, please visit: www.routledge.com/ Routledge-New-Directions-in-PR--Communication-Research/book-series/ RNDPRCR

Financial Communication
A Critical Assessment

Keith Butterick

Routledge
Taylor & Francis Group

LONDON AND NEW YORK

First published 2025
by Routledge
4 Park Square, Milton Park, Abingdon, Oxon OX14 4RN

and by Routledge
605 Third Avenue, New York, NY 10158

Routledge is an imprint of the Taylor & Francis Group, an informa business

© 2025 Keith Butterick

British Library Cataloguing-in-Publication Data
A catalogue record for this book is available from the British Library

ISBN: 978-0-367-34038-4 (hbk)
ISBN: 978-1-032-97575-7 (pbk)
ISBN: 978-0-429-32358-4 (ebk)

DOI: 10.4324/9780429323584

Typeset in Times New Roman
by codeMantra

Contents

Preface

The communication between a public company, its existing shareholders and potential investors is one of the most important functions it has to fulfil to meet not just investor perception but regulatory requirements. While this is driven by the need to respond to regulation, there is another compelling reason why a public company communicates with the shareholders: they are its owners.

The communication is carried out on behalf of the public company by communication professionals. This book is about this specialised form of communication.

For many years I worked on financial public relations (PR), focusing on the flotations of public companies, contested takeovers, mergers and acquisitions. Then, there were two distinct but complementary aspects, financial PR which dealt with media relations and communications such as producing the company annual report. The second element was investor relations (IR) dealing with the specific communication between the company and its existing shareholders; in some cases, this was done by the financial PR company but in many cases by specialist IR practitioners, usually with a finance background.

However, the USA academic, Dr. Alexander Laskin puts a different interpretation on the practice; financial PR is regarded as an earlier form of the practice but now superseded by IR. Dr. Laskin is a noted and respected academic with many publications to his credit and has done a great deal to raise the status of research into financial communications (this is my preferred term for financial PR and IR). As one of the, if not the leading scholar in this field his opinions carry weight, his history of how the practice developed has been quoted and used by other writers on the subject. It is fair to say that his interpretation of financial communications has become the dominant paradigm in the field, quoted and referred to by other academics.

As a former practitioner, I knew that his interpretation, at least as far as the UK was concerned, was wrong. This book started as a challenge to this paradigm based on the historical evidence on how the practice developed in the UK and the USA.

However, to present a complete picture, I realised I had to go further and each chapter reflects this. Chapter 1 includes a history of the public company demonstrating that communication between the company and its shareholders has been a feature since the 16th century. Chapter 2 considers the communication channels used by the public company to communicate with shareholders and potential shareholders and how this continues to shape the nature of the communication. This chapter also covers how financial communication has grown and the very different origins in the UK and the USA.

Chapter 3 considers the question of what a paradigm is and how these become established in different disciplines. This is because Dr. Laskin has a broader aim than establishing a dominant paradigm in financial communications and that is to 'prove' that the excellence theory developed by James Grunig works in practice.

Furthermore, as he deliberately associates his model with a specific ideology, the efficient market hypothesis, this led me to consider an under-researched field in PR, the role of ideology.

No one can write about financial communications without considering the role of shareholders in the public company. They are the owners of the company, but what much of the literature does not seem to recognise is how the nature of shareholders is changing, along with how the shares are bought and sold. Information from the company to its shareholders has always been crucial to buying and selling shares. Chapter 4 is a detailed analysis of these issues along with the lessons of contemporary events such as GameStop.

That Dr. Laskin's model of financial communications supports a market-based philosophy at a time when many public companies are recognising the importance of issues such as the environment and how to involve more stakeholders led me to consider what role could financial communications play in encouraging attitudes to change. Chapter 5 is a short contribution to what should be a growing debate. While I suggest critical PR could be a basis for this, it also recognises that it does not yet provide all the answers if, indeed, it ever could.

Acknowledgements

Particular thanks for help in this project go to Kevin Moloney for suggesting my original idea might be worth pursuing, Aimee Calvert for all her assistance, Alex Atkinson of Routledge for encouragement and understanding, Dr. Deidre O'Neill for her comments on the text, critical advice and friendship and finally Lorna, yet again for her patience.

1   Historical origins

Joint-stock companies

The basic features of the modern public company emerged in the middle of the 16th century when two existing structures, the partnership and the corporation, were fused together to become the joint-stock company. Joint-stock companies, like the modern public company, were vehicles to raise money from investors outside of the company to expand it. In the 16th century they were ideal to fund speculative and risky ventures to develop trade with the new territories recently opened for European traders. The first joint-stock companies were the Russia Company (1553), the East India Company, the Hudson Bay Company (1668), Virginia (1606), Bermuda (1611), Guyana (1619), New England (1620) and Nova Scotia (1621). They could only raise money from potential investors if they had a Crown Charter, and their number was strictly controlled with the sale of the shares to investors through private negotiation. The Charter system not only restricted the number of companies but also the growth of specialist brokers who traded in company shares. In 1602, The Dutch East India Company became the first company to sell shares in the business to the public.

Charters were also granted to companies in the UK who were looking to expand and grow their business. In 1568, for example, a Charter was awarded to the Company of the Mines Royal and the Mineral & Battery Company, which needed funds to develop new production methods. In fact, this is a prime example of why companies even now turn to external investors for finance – to fund expansion or invest in new technology that cannot be funded by the company internally.

The joint-stock company was, however, even from its earliest manifestations, regarded with suspicion because it provided an opportunity for the unscrupulous to rob the unwary through the creation of false companies and dubious investment schemes. To prevent such fraudulent and illegal activity legislation was introduced to control their activities. This legislation and the need to respond and explain the actions of companies to their stakeholders have been factors in the growth of investor relations. From the 1720 Bubble

DOI: 10.4324/9780429323584-1

Act, which restricted the creation of joint-stock companies for over a century to the latest version of the Companies Act in 2006, governments legislated to prevent or correct fraudulent corporate activities.

Lies, corruption, financial newspapers and financial communication

There has always been a close, symbiotic relationship between companies and the communication channels of the day – a characteristic that continues down to the present. The communication channel is the means through which the company communicates to its target audiences. A feature of 21st-century communication is the way this is becoming less mediated through third parties such as traditional print media with companies communicating directly with their audience through the internet. This offers not only the opportunity of direct communication with an audience, but also, crucially, enables feedback from them.

Financial journalism is one of the oldest forms of journalism. The first financial newspaper was published in Antwerp by the trading house of Van der Molen in 1540 (McCusker, 1991; Butterick, 2015). While it might not have the recognition of, for example, political, sports or foreign journalism, it has nevertheless been hugely important to the business of journalism, generating substantial advertising and commercial revenues for newspapers and magazines. It has also played an important role in legitimising economic and political ideologies.

When London replaced Antwerp as the financial capital of Europe in the early 18th century it developed its own unique news distribution network, the London coffee houses. At the beginning of the 18th-century London had over 2000 coffee houses[1] individual houses were associated with a particular clientele or profession. Investors and potential investors in companies used this network to gather information on businesses and trading conditions that might affect their investment. Two coffee houses, Jonathans and Lloyds, had a long-term impact not only on financial journalism but also on London's financial history. Edward Lloyd opened his first coffee house in 1687 near London's docks. With its mercantile and shipping connections, Lloyds became the headquarters for a profession that became known as marine 'underwriters'[2] (Dale, 2004). In 1691 Lloyd moved his establishment to Lombard Street to be nearer to the General Post Office, then an important source of shipping information (Kynaston, 1994).

The availability of newspapers in the coffee houses was an important attraction to customers and coffee houses started producing their own newspapers to provide better information than the newspapers of the day. Edward Lloyd's, *Lloyds List* contained news and information on shipping issues and became so valuable and accurate that after his death in 1713, customers of the coffee house took over its publication. Both Lloyds and *Lloyds List* still exist, Lloyds being the home for UK insurance underwriters, *Lloyds List* is currently owned by the Informa Group and although now an online publication, it still covers insurance related matters.

Jonathan's coffee house was established by Jonathan Miles in Exchange Alley in 1680 (Kynaston, 1994) attracting customers involved or associated with the buying and selling of company shares. The attraction of the newspaper produced by Jonathan's was that it provided regular and up-to-date commercial news on for example, lost cargoes, problems of diseased crews and delays in sailing caused by repairs to a ship – essentially any news that might impact on a trading mission. Miles went to great lengths to gather the information and deliver it faster than his rivals, he had an army of boys waiting around London's docks for ships to arrive and pick up relevant stories. Their collective findings were displayed on boards inside the coffee house (Dale, 2004; Roush, 2006; Butterick, 2015).

The Observer newspaper began reporting on 'City' matters in 1820 a feature subsequently adopted by other newspapers. The title 'father of financial journalism' goes to Thomas Masa Alsager, the City Editor of *The Times* (Porter, 2004). Historical events such as the so-called railway mania of the 1830s highlights a recurring dichotomy newspapers of the day and modern online media continue to grapple with. For *The Times*, the country's leading newspaper in the 1830s, the advertisements from railway companies publicising forthcoming flotations of railway companies was a lucrative income. It was, however, not only national newspapers such as *The Times* that benefitted from railway advertising; provincial newspapers such as the *Leeds Mercury* from where the Brontes drew information for their investments (Butterick, 2015) also attracted railway advertisements which were important source of information about the railway companies.

The age-old dichotomy for the media however, is how critical or supportive they should be of the industry or company they are writing about. In railway mania for example, *The Times* and its City Editor, Thomas Masa Alsager, maintained their journalistic independence and credibility when they contributed to bursting the railway share bubble through questioning whether the investments in the railways had any long-term value. This caused the share price of many railway companies to fall.

If Alsager represents credible financial journalism, at the other end of the spectrum are the so-called City Slickers who were financial journalists at the *Daily Mirror* in the late 1990s. James Hipwell and Anil Bhoyrul wrote about companies in which they owned shares with the intention of pushing the share price higher so they gained financially. This continues to be a problem with financial journalism: many, for example, believe that the ruthless promotion of property ownership in the media contributed to hyping the property buying that led to the financial crash of 2008[3]

In 1898 Salomon Van Oss argued,

> Those who have shares to unload can well afford to give needy or unscrupulous journalists an inducement; and after seeing a number of paragraphs in newspapers praising up certain shares of which he knows nothing, many an investor decides to put his money into what afterwards proves to be a foredoomed concern. Investors have such a childlike faith in anything that is printed!
>
> (Van Oss in Butterick, 2015: 39).

Charles Duguid (1902: 39), the City editor of the *Daily Mail* and one of the most important figures in the history of financial journalism, highlights how journalists attempt to balance their editorial between the two conflicting pressures, the commercial and the critical editorial:

> Sometimes there will be found on the same money page one of these colourless notices and, on another part of the page, a criticism of the prospectus as well. The one is the customary concession to the advertiser or to the advertising agent; the other is the expression of the opinion of the paper for the benefit of the reader. But as a general rule the money articles of the great morning papers contain the colourless prospectus notice alone.

Industrialisation in the UK of the 1870s and 1880s led to a huge rise in the number of companies going public and created a share bubble, which, as with other financial bubbles, attracted the attention of inexperienced investors. To their rescue came the *Daily Mail*, the newspaper created to articulate the views and reflect the interests of the urban class created by industrialisation.

While the *Daily Mail's* founder Alfred Harmsworth saw financial journalism as a commercial proposition to attract advertising, he believed that readers who invested in stocks and shares – clerks, office workers, shopkeepers and middle managers – would not only receive a welcome financial return, but would also enhance their social status. Harmsworth though accepted that by offering investment advice, the newspaper also had a responsibility to new inexperienced investors and so developed a new style of financial journalism to both encourage and assist.

The newspaper laid out its position in its column 'Advice to Investors':

> The wants of the small investor will receive particular notice. We will explain technicalities to those who do not understand them. We shall endeavour to interpose between the inexperienced and the loss of their money; but they must get in the way of asking our advice before they act. Investors frequently fall into trouble first and ask advice afterwards. We shall of course do the best we can for all: but if they will seek counsel before they invest it will be better for them.
>
> (*Daily Mail*, 4 May 1896)

Although changes to company law during the 1850s and 1860s had provided more security to shareholders, the way shares were offered remained broadly the same in the 1880s as in the South Sea Bubble in 1720. Investors bought shares based on information provided by the companies, with little or no external check on the veracity or accuracy of that information.

An historian of 19th-century financial journalism, writing in 1904, describes in detail the problems facing investors at the time:

> Investors had great difficulty in obtaining trustworthy information about the securities in which their money was embarked. The Money articles of the general newspapers were chiefly taken up with the bare records of movements in the Funds, foreign stocks, and English railway securities. About the various American railways, Erie, Wabash, Central Pacific – in which millions of English capital were invested – they had no information except that which was contained in the inspired memoranda sent to them from time to time by the London agents of the American directors, which was frequently stale and sometimes misleading.
>
> (Kynaston, 1994: 4)

This issue of how to get the right type of information continues to affect share buying in the 21st century. At every stage of the sale process the parties involved had a vested interest in promoting the interests of the company and attempting to push the share price up, with the concerns of the shareholder a secondary consideration. Stockbrokers, for example, took a commission on the sale of company shares so their advice was compromised. Company promoters and share pushers who promoted shares to the public had little or no regulation over their activities or the claims they made. Opportunities for unscrupulous, crooked share promotions and bogus schemes were rife. In many ways the company promoters and share pushers were the forerunners of the modern financial PR practitioners.

Not all journalists at this time were as principled as the *Daily Mail*'s Duguid. In 1898, for example, the magazine *Nineteenth Century* complained,

> That the City has a large number of 'reptile' journals, which will praise – and for that matter also condemn – anything as long as they are paid for it, is by this time well known to anyone who is not a tyro in finance. But unfortunately, investors are mostly tyros in finance.
>
> (Robb, 2002: 117)

Duguid and other financial journalists of the period were attempting to produce a code of practice for financial writers by defining what their roles and responsibilities should be. The ideal City editor, according to Duguid, should practice a code that would mean being: "Assiduous in collecting his financial facts, level-headed in appraising them, precise in arraying them." He should be prepared to express "a definite opinion on his facts" which should be delivered with "honesty and rectitude." The emphasis in the proposed code was the professionalism and integrity of the journalist (Porter, 1998: 54). Duguid also suggests the financial journalist should act in a similar fashion to a magistrate when considering evidence: disinterested and capable of arriving at an independent judgement.

Reflecting on the differences between the new and old types of journalism, Duguid said that the, "Older form of financial journalism" was boring and uninteresting,

> With a dull coldness, [it] set forth mere price movements, without embellishment, hint or explanation of any kind. There was little danger that readers would be misled; neither it was to be said, was there much danger that they would be usefully informed.
>
> (Porter, 1998: 50)

The new financial journalism, however, was according to Duguid, characterised by "crisp" and "outspoken" commentary, "successful tips" and "trenchant disclosure of financial fraud" (Porter, 1998: 50). The success of the new financial journalism had, he said, "Been evinced over and over again...the wiles of the unscrupulous company promoter have been laid bare, and hundreds and thousands of pounds have been retained in the pocket of the thrifty investor."

This continues to be a balance that the UK and US media attempt to maintain. However, few modern financial journalists see their role as that of watchdogs. Tambini (2010: 172) demonstrates how PR now plays a "powerful" role in the financial media with few City journalists believing they have what he describes as a "corporate governance role" that is one of, "Providing the balanced and sceptical news and comment that deflates bubbles and helps avoid market irrationality" as Duguid demanded. While the financial journalists in Tambini's survey tended to agree on the key challenges they face, they are uncertain how to respond to them.

Journalists such as Duguid were not critics of the system rather they wanted to make it operate efficiently and effectively by removing the crooks. The quality of their writing, however, raised the standard of financial journalism, turning it into a source of information that by and large could be trusted. However, they also contributed to social change, their contributions normalised share ownership and made it acceptable for a whole new class. This lasting significance was ideological: "Late nineteenth-century financial journalists were effectively popularizing capitalism, facilitating the spread of share ownership amongst their readers. Along with this came an enhanced awareness of the particular responsibilities attached to financial journalism as an occupation or profession" (Parsons, 1989: 22). They were crucial in legitimising "economic values, ideas and language" (Poovey, 2002: 34). They normalised the market and the activities of the joint-stock company and brought them into common use through discussion and comment and helped market operations appear to be, "a law-governed, natural, and – pre-eminently – safe sector of modern society" (Poovey, 2002: 34). Preda (2009) sees the mid-19th century as a turning point helping to overcome the suspicions surrounding the joint-stock company, the old way of seeing financial speculation as gambling gave way to a new form of "science of financial investments" which stressed rationality and downplayed human agency. This new scientific vision "promoted the notion that financial markets are governed by principles which are not controlled by any single individual or group. Even if some persons may occasionally manipulate markets, these principles will ultimately prevail." Market activity was made "socially legitimate and morally acceptable" and large numbers of investors were by these means incorporated into the market (Preda, 2009: 86).

Media influence on share buying

The question of how much influence the media has on share buying, especially with retail investors continues to be widely debated.

Schiller (2000) argues that:

> The role of the news media in the stock market is not, as commonly believed, simply as a convenient tool for investors who are reacting directly to the economically significant news itself. The media actively shape public attention and categories of thought and they create the environment within which the stock market events we see are played out.

Bhattacharya et al (2009) demonstrate that in the 'dot-com' bubble during the late 1990s media 'hype' contributed to the febrile excitement in the bubble period. The focus of the media attention being on those shares that rose the highest.[4] Engellberg and Parsons (2011) found that retail investors in the United States tended to buy local shares featured in local newspapers. In the UK the decimation of local newspapers and their coverage of business make these an unlikely source of influence.

A problem for many public companies however, is that what impacts on the share price can often be coverage of a non-stock market problem that affects a company's reputation but over which they may not have a great deal of influence. This hits the sales figures, which in turn leads to a falling share price. In 2008 British Airways (BA) opened a state-of-the-art passenger terminal at Heathrow Airport; the company claimed it had learned lessons from previous airport openings that had gone wrong (Denver, 1995; Madrid, 1994). However, on the opening day there was chaos, caused through simple and avoidable errors. BA employees for instance, could not park their cars in staff car parks or get through security. There were also further problems in baggage handling despite having put the baggage handlers through a rigorous training programme. The cost to BA of the opening day chaos was £16 million, the BA share price fell 3% on the opening day, wiping £90 million off BA's value. This is an illustration of how random events, despite the years BA spent planning and preparing for the opening, can impact on the share price.

Arfin (1994: 24) argues, "Everyone acknowledges that the financial media has an influential role, but interestingly, with the exception it plays in reaching investors, no-one will say what that role is."

Nowadays the potential investor has a range of investment advice driven by changing technology. In the US for example, there are a number of dedicated TV channels where traders and investors can access information, Bloomberg TV is available on the internet and in the UK. The *Wall Street Journal* has, like many other newspapers diversified into its own dedicated TV channel similar channels have been launched by the *Financial Times*, *Forbes*, *The Economist*, and *Barrons*. There are dedicated channels for financial news such as CNN Money and Fox Business. In addition, there are any number of podcasts by commentators, websites and internet sites that share information, comments and recommendations between investors.

The internet provides the opportunity of direct communication between a public company and its audiences. Public companies use their websites to include a dedicated section for their shareholders, with information such as media announcements and directors' statements relevant to investors. More sophisticated sites will have dedicated investor TV channels and podcasts, or films of the AGM.

While investors can access a range of information on potential investments mobile phone trading enables information not only to be despatched immediately but also to trade immediately on that information. However, for all the access to this information and ease of trading, research by Gurrola-Perez et al (2002: 56) illustrate that the concerns of Duguid and Harmsworth remain important and need to be addressed. Their research among stock exchanges throughout the world demonstrated that, "Without minimum levels of financial literacy and education, retail investors may be easily driven into misleading investment strategies. If lacking adequate protection, investors may fall victims to financial scams." Arfin (1994: 43) also supports the education role arguing that: "A large part of a financial communicators' job is educational, ensuring that the media are kept up to date and negatives put in context."

Gurrola-Perez et al (2002) found retail participants in the market tend to react to market conditions, which they learn from external sources such as the media, blogs and web comments. Trade in shares is higher after potential purchasers have seen high market returns and they trade less when market volatilities are high, demonstrating their uncertainty.

Evidence from a number of different sources suggests that journalists do influence the buying and selling of shares. Campbek et al (2012: 641) for example, confirms the impact journalists have on retail investors: "The writing

of a specific journalist has a *causal* effect on aggregate market outcomes."
The authors go on to say:

> Our results suggest that financial journalists have the potential to influence
> investor behaviour, at least over short time horizons. The role of finan-
> cial journalists is ultimately to provide color and interpretation to market
> events, we would expect their effects to be highest around news events and
> volatile returns. In contrast, evidence on the limited attention of investors
> might suggest that investors are least persuadable during these busy peri-
> ods and, therefore financial journalism might matter in 'quieter' times. Fi-
> nancial journalism appears to causally influence stock returns, even more
> so during times of extreme market sentiment.

Barber and Odean (2007) confirm that retail investors are, "buyers of
attention-grabbing stocks – eg stocks in the news, stocks experiencing high
abnormal trading volume and stocks with extreme one-day returns." They
also find that there is evidence that trading (in shares), "increases on days with
information releases (by companies)."

Johnson-Young et al (2005) demonstrate that negative articles in the news
on questions of for example, corporate governance can also influence the
share price, with investors more likely to sell shares in a company that is
perceived negatively because it is perceived to be poorly managed. Tetlock
(2007: 3554) argues that "pessimistic media content" predicts downward
pressure on market prices.

Large public companies which are usually household names employing
thousands have always been able to generate media coverage on their activities. Small cap companies, even though they may be substantial employers
in terms of the number of people they employ, have traditionally struggled to
gain satisfactory coverage from either the media or analysts. The [5]internet and
direct communication with their target audience has provided a major boost
to their communications.

Despite the limitations on their role and decline in numbers, financial journalists still retain an important function – they are relied on by investors and
the public to filter or assess the 'investability' of companies; offering buy and
sell advice; comment on trading news and financial results, and making sense
of complex financial information. Dougal et al (2012: 670) state that, "direct
evidence that the writing of specific journalists has a causal effect on aggregate outcomes of investor actions."

Financial journalists however, also remain subject to those attempting to
influence their story or the way it is framed. While Tambini highlights the
influence PR has on financial journalists, Lee (2014) demonstrates that while
financial journalists are 'active agents' in shaping public opinion they rely for
their information from, 'financial professionals, government officials, that is

because the news they are producing is not meant for wider public interest but investors and other businesspeople.' In addition, financial reporting is 'challenging' because it relies on press releases from the companies being written about fast-moving complex information. There is also a danger that beat reporters, that is special reporters who cover a specific sector such as banking for example, have too close a relationship with their sources, which may stifle critical stories (Butterick, 2015).

Whether through the traditional print/broadcast media or through new sources such as mobile phones, traditional financial PR continue to have an important role.

Notes

1 They epitomised the 'public sphere' a place where open and free debate between citizens' could and did take place.

2 So-called because they wrote their names under the terms of the insurance contract to show they accepted the risks associated with the policy.

3 Ironically, Alsager was fired from *The Times* for promoting the shares of a west country rail company that he had shares in.

4 The so-called 'dot-com' bubble had all the characteristics of earlier bubbles. Businesses fuelled by venture capital companies and private investors new businesses opened to take advantage of the internet. At its height the Nasdaq rose to 400% only to fall by 78% losing all the gains. Unlike current online activity, consumers/business purchasers were not used to buying online.

5 In the US a small cap company is one with a total market value or market capitalisation from $250 million to $2 billion, In the UK the valuation is up to £35 million.

2 Growth of financial communications

Historical background

The advertising of legitimate company prospectuses has always been a valid form of promotion, share promoters have also used more dubious methods to promote company shares. For example, in the summer of 1720 the South Sea Company attempted to keep the share price as high as possible to attract new investors to pay dividends to the original investors. To demonstrate how little changes in the 21st century, maintaining or sustaining a company's share price in order to pay dividends to shareholders is regarded as one of the most important obligations of a public company by their shareholders.

The South Sea Company directors deliberately spread false stories and rumours such as, for example, that a free trade agreement between England and Spain was imminent, and that Mexico would trade all the gold in its mines for English cotton and woollen goods. They also stated that for every £100 invested in the company, investors would receive hundreds of pounds of dividends every year. These stories were little more than deliberate attempts to try and shape share buying perception and increase excitement around the shares. Without a trading performance this could not be maintained, and from a high point in the summer of 1720 when the shares reached £890 per share the price collapsed to £150 per share (Butterick, 2015). Despite rumours and falsehoods at some point a company has to deliver financial returns for investors.

The pattern of buying and selling shares was for many years a straightforward process with two separate elements. The share purchaser went to a stockbroker who, acting on their behalf bought shares from a stock jobber acting for the company. The principle on which business was transacted was 'trust' – between the client and between the partners who were jointly and severally liable for each other's debts, so the principle of 'my word is my bond' mattered. Both brokers and jobbers worked on a fixed commission. Responsibility for 'promoting' or 'pushing' the shares fell to the jobber. Because there was so much secrecy surrounding their role they were viewed with suspicion by the investing public. As late as 1908 the *Financial Times* observed

DOI: 10.4324/9780429323584-2

that jobbers had "a reputation which is a by-word for all that is reprehensible" (Attard, 1994: 44).

Stockbrokers charged a fixed commission for their services and while this produced a good living for the small band of elite traders it was an almost amateurish way of operating with typical late starts at 10:00 am and long alcohol-fuelled lunches. The City of London was seen as an extended 'gentlemen's club'[1] only accessed by the socially privileged and the well-connected (Jeremy, 1998). As the fixed commission was the main source of income there was no incentive for stockbrokers to try and create corporate activity or to increase their fees by making deals through, for example, the takeover of one public company by another. When Initial Public Offerings (IPO's, also known as flotations or going public) occurred, they were relatively modest in size.

During the 1950s and 1960s the City of London was an insular, hermetic world where staff recruitment to the main financial institutions that traditionally define 'the City' (the stockbrokers and merchant banks) was dominated by the old-boy school network, where social contacts and connections arguably mattered more than talent. The boardrooms of many public companies contained peers of the realm, not necessarily because they knew anything about business but because their social contacts opened doors for companies into the City. A peer on the board provided the company with the appearance of solidity and respectability (Jeremy, 1998).

The first financial PR consultancies in the UK and US

Arfin (1994: 5) notes that, "Before Big Bang in the late 1980s, most companies relied on their brokers or merchant bankers for a good deal of communication advice and informed investor relations. Financial PR, if used at all, were employed for media management." Often their role was keeping the company's name out of the financial pages as much as attempting to gain coverage.

This was the background against which the UK's first financial PR company, John Addey Associates, was launched in 1970. In an environment where personal relationships dominated, communication with the media was seen as neither relevant nor important for most established public companies. John Addey was the UK's first recognised financial PR practitioner, and the ideal operator for the clubbable network of pre-Big Bang City of London. A former barrister, he understood that to succeed in this environment he needed the correct image and cultivated his meticulously. He was, for example, always immaculately groomed, employed a butler and drove to business meetings in a Bentley convertible. His style of doing business was perfectly suited to the 'City way' of using extensive personal City and media contacts (Coyle, 2004).

John Coyle, then a journalist, (2004) recalls how he first met Addey: "The telephone call came out of the blue from a man I had never met nor spoken to before. In fact I had never heard of him. I was working as a staff writer for the financial pages of a national Sunday newspaper." He said, "John, I am the public relations consultant to a well-known financier and would dearly love to talk to you about him. Could you spare some time to have dinner with me at the Savoy?" As an intrigued Coyle had never met anyone in public relations before, he accepted the invitation: "The dinner was lavish, the benefactor was enthusiastic and, as I recall, the waiter was tipped £10 for doing little more than supply vast amounts of expensive alcohol." An impression was clearly made on Coyle, as he went on to become one of the most important financial PR consultants in the UK in the 1980s. This incident also illustrates the career progression of many financial journalists at the time, from journalism into the emerging world of financial public relations.

With media coverage a low priority for public companies at this time and with few regulatory obligations requiring them to disclose information, public companies distributed only limited amounts of information to financial journalists. Press releases, for example, when they were issued were delivered by hand to journalists who had little formal opportunity to follow up on a release or ask questions of company executives. There was limited contextual information available, as few stockbrokers provided research that enabled comparisons to be made between the performances of different companies. The value and worth of a company could only be assessed through the published financial figures such as the profits or losses the company had made, the dividends paid out, and the share performance over the long term. This situation, however, was ideal for a practitioner such as John Addey who could and did shape media opinion through his personal influence and contacts with journalists.

Tim Jackaman of Square Mile Communications said of Addey,

As far as I'm concerned, all the thoroughbred horses in this industry have come from one stallion... and that stallion is John Addey. He really invented the whole genre of financial PR. He was a very successful chap, as sharp as anything and charming, too. Importantly, he had a good head for figures and ran a line between clients and journalists brilliantly. In his heyday he was a colossus.

(Blackhurst, 2000: 15)

While investing in stock shares had a long tradition in the UK, in the United States it was only at the start of the 20th century that buying company securities became popular with retail investors as the economic boom in manufacturing and railway industries saw the emergence of large companies eager to expand and needing finance from outsiders investors to do so. A growing, cash-rich middle class had developed looking to invest in new opportunities. The contrasting situations of the US and UK reflect the different stages in their economic growth. In the US, as in the UK, there were also fraudulent schemes that robbed investors (Macey and Miller, 1993: 394). Speculative securities were often sold by door-to-door salesmen. Macey and Miller quoting a banking journal stated that, "So many people have lost their money on 'fake' investment that they seem to be incapable of distinguishing the false from the genuine, and hence are distrustful of all" (Macey and Miller, 1991: 394). How many times have similar comments been made about joint stock companies?

The Second World War affected the US and UK economies differently and also determined how financial communication in both countries developed. In the UK, the government, faced with a need to reconstruct the economy and the country's infrastructure damaged by the war, imposed restrictions on how companies could distribute their profits, requiring them to re-invest in new plant and factories rather than give dividends to shareholders. A post-war consumer boom did not materialise until the late 1950s.

In the US, by contrast, there was an almost immediate post-war boom as the economy emerged as the strongest in the world. Cash-rich consumers with money were drawn to invest in public companies by the promise of strong dividend growth. Individual investors in US grew rapidly, from 4.5 million in 1958 to over 20 million in 1965. Consequently, financial communication in the US during the 1950s was built around companies communicating their share offers to the new, potential shareholders. It was to the then embryonic public relations consultancies that corporations turned to complement their in-house departments. Investor relations was viewed as an extension of the public relations function. Companies began to employ personnel to manage the communication with increasing numbers of shareholders. The first in-house function in the US to manage all of the company's shareholder communications was established in 1953 by Ralph Cordiner, the Chairman of General Electric.

Financial PR, Big Bang and de-regulation

The different economic and regulatory environment in the UK and USA also influenced the development and growth of financial communications. In 1986 the safe, comfortable, closed world of the City in London was shattered by a series of regulatory changes known as Big Bang. An unintended consequence of this was to give the financial PR industry a major boost. Although Big Bang is principally identified with the Conservative administration of Mrs Thatcher, the idea that the City needing freeing from closed restrictive practices circulated amongst politicians for a number of years (Jeremy, 1998).

The regulatory changes affected and transformed, not only the City, but also the whole financial services sector. Competition was introduced into the previously closed world of the building societies, enabling them to compete with banks and allowing them to expand their range of services by offering current accounts in addition to savings accounts. Banks were allowed to compete with the building societies in the home lending market by offering mortgages. Restrictions on borrowing were removed which would lead in the future to the UK having high levels of both corporate and personal debt. These are also the historical roots of the 2008 financial crisis (Jeremy, 1998; Hutton, 1995).

In the City, the restrictions separating jobbers from brokers were removed, allowing the development of so-called 'integrated' house banks while other financial institutions were allowed to buy brokers and jobbers firms or establish their own. Freeing the market allowed foreign financial institutions the opportunity to buy into London firms, transforming not only the way that business was conducted but also perhaps more importantly the whole business culture (Jeremy, 1998).

London's financial services industry became dominated by a small number of large, powerful banks largely controlled by US or Swiss financial institutions. Foreign ownership brought with it not only new management and funds to finance large transactions, but crucially a different and more aggressive culture. Out, for example, went fixed commission remuneration to be replaced by a bonus culture driven by personal motivation. Success in deals such as contested takeovers, mergers and IPOs were incentivised by bonuses, resulting in personal rewards through large bonus payments. Kay Review (2012: 18) summarised the changes brought about by Big Bang:

> The norms of the City of London were significantly affected by the pre-eminent role established by US investment banks, which favoured transactions and trading over relationships, and whose style was imitated by their European counterparts. This cultural shift was associated with a rapid rise in share prices 1982–2000.

The rise in aggressive merger and acquisition activity, including hostile takeovers, put the management of public companies under pressure and in the spotlight: "Very quickly, in-depth, strategic communication became vital." (Arfin, 1994: 6).

The US did not experience similar financial de-regulation or market stimulation created by selling former state-controlled assets such as gas, electricity and water companies. In the UK financial PR developed out of the needs of growing corporations while privatisation and IPOs drove the growth of IR. In contrast, USA financial PR was driven by the growth in social activism and the need for companies to respond to outsiders (Hayagreeva and Sivakumar, 1999).

The combination of financial institutions with access to larger amounts of capital and a rising stock market, meant finance was available for companies who wanted to do deals such as takeovers. As remuneration for executives at the City's merchant banks and stockbrokers became increasingly transaction driven, teams at the corporate finance departments in accountants, merchant banks became proactive. Instead of waiting for deals to come in to them they searched public and private companies looking for potential deals, approaching companies to try and 'sell' them the deal. The type of transactions included private companies going public through a stock market listing or existing quoted companies using their shares to expand by acquiring other companies though agreed or contested mergers and acquisitions.

The resulting flurry of flotations, privatisations, or takeovers, whether contested or agreed, required the communication process to be managed properly and professionally because takeover battles were fought out in the public eye through the media (Davis, 2006). Contested takeover bids made excellent newspaper copy, enlivening the sometimes dry and repetitive copy of financial and business journalism. This was especially true when the battle was reduced to an assessment about the contrasting management styles of the two opposing chief executives. Stories were sometimes spiced by salacious personal details of the characters involved. In its early days for the emerging financial PR industry the ability to access the financial and business pages of the key national newspapers was the main requirement; therefore the employment of ex-financial journalists such as Coyle became key to their services. The media became increasingly important in determining the outcome of these takeovers, which meant that controlling and managing media communication became crucial in determining the outcome of a bid (Butterick, 2015)

As financial PR developed in the UK, specialists emerged catering for different business sectors. Some firms concentrated on the flotations of the former utilities and large financial institutions such as the Halifax Building Society. Others, such as Brunswick, specialised in contested takeovers while some specialised in the IPO's of small companies. The growing stock market during the 1980s encouraged several smaller companies to float on the stock market, either to realise value for shareholders or to raise new capital to grow the business. Binns Cornwall, founded in 1980, was a specialist in the IPO's of small companies and at its height had 178 clients.

Dewe Rogerson was the financial PR company that handled the most privatisations on behalf of the UK government and was responsible for approximately 90% of the privatisations. Starting with the BT campaign it went on to handle the privatisations of Britoil, British Gas, TSB, BP, British Steel and the water and electricity industries. Many criticised the government of the day for putting so much power into the hands of one firm, which was not only responsible for the financial PR but also choosing the advertising agencies (Chapman, 2011). Now part of Citigate Dewe Rogerson, which handles a broader range of work than IPOs it continues with similar work handling the flotation of the Royal Mail in 2013.

One of the most successful of the companies specialising in mergers and acquisitions in the 1980s was Broad Street Associates founded by Brian Basham, a protégé of John Addey. Basham had been a financial journalist at the *Daily Mail*, the *Daily Telegraph* and *The Times*, joining John Addey Associates in 1972 leaving in 1976 to form Broad Street Associates with John Coyle (the journalist wined and dined by Addey). Broad Street itself eventually became a public company with a turnover of £15 million. As Addey defined financial PR in the 1970s, so Basham and Coyle's Broad Street defined financial PR in the 1980s, developing a reputation for high-profile and aggressive PR.

Basham's "trademark was carrying out detailed investigations of his opponents' strengths and weaknesses which were then used in the takeover" (Blackhurst, 2000: 16). As specialists in the hostile takeover, Basham and Coyle were involved in almost all the big deals of the time such as the Hanson and United Biscuits' bid for Imperial Group and Argyll's unsuccessful battle with Guinness for Distillers.

Modern financial PR practitioners used dubious tactics some similar to those used by their forerunners at the South Sea Company in 1720. In 1995, for example, during a disputed takeover between the construction company Amec and the company bidding for it, the Norwegian shipping company Kvaerner, the financial PR company acting on behalf of Amec was censured by the Takeover Panel for leaking price-sensitive information about it to the media concerning profit expectations. This breached the Takeover Code of the day. Once again we can see echoes of tactics that have been used throughout history.

One of the most notorious tactics used by financial PR companies was the so-called "Friday night drop." Its purpose was simple, to try and influence the financial headlines in the Sunday newspapers and especially the *Sunday Times* and *Sunday Telegraph*. It was believed this would set the media agenda for the rest of the week. The practice, which was eventually outlawed by the Financial Services Authority, involved a financial PR consultant phoning a newspaper contact on Friday evening and offering them an unaccredited exclusive. This could range from leaking a favourable stockbrokers report on a client, to information on a possible takeover target. The rationale, rightly or wrongly, was that Sunday was the one day that key influencers had time to read a story. Sometimes the story used information that bordered on insider trading (Butterick, 2015).

Investor relations

A recurring problem for public relations has been the inability to provide a common definition of what it is, while there have been numerous efforts – one estimate is that there are 54 attempts to provide a clear-cut explanation. Definitions however, become marginally easier in specific sectors such as consumer and trade PR. Financial PR also used to have a straightforward definition – the communication carried out either in-house or by an external PR consultancy to undertake communications on behalf of a public company. Investor Relations was a separate but related activity usually carried out in-house or by specialist companies to handle the relation between current and potential shareholders.

Investor relations sets out to provide present and potential investors with an accurate portrayal of a company's performance and prospects.

> By investor relations we mean continuous, planned, deliberate, sustained marketing activities that identify, establish, maintain and enhance both long and short-term relationships between a company and not only its prospective and present investors, but also other financial analysts and stakeholders.
>
> (Dolphin, 2004: 26)

The UK Investor Relations Society defines the practice as,

> The communication of information and insight between a company and the investment community. This process enables a full appreciation of the company's business activities, strategy and prospects and allows the market to make an informed judgement about the fair value and appropriate ownership of a company.

The definition of IR by the USA National Investor Relations Institute (NIRI) adopted in 2003 defines IR as

> a strategic management responsibility that integrates finance, communication, Marketing and securities law compliance to enable the most effective two-way communication between a company, the financial community, and other constituencies, which ultimately contributes to a company's securities achieving a fair valuation.

The London Stock Exchange Guide to Listing (2022: 28), describes investor relations as,

> the ongoing activity of companies communication with the investment community. While the communication that companies undertake is a mix of regulatory and voluntary activities. IR is essentially the part of public life that sees companies interacting with shareholders, potential investors, research analysts and journalists. Large companies frequently create a separate IR function to meet the demands for information and to assist in all communications with the market.

According to Marston (1996: 478), "Investor Relations can be defined as the link between a company and the financial community, providing information to help the financial community and investing public evaluate a company." Crucially, Marston argues investor relations is not a neutral process restricted to providing information to assist customers: "IR may also be concerned with managing information flows in the best interests of the company" (1996: 478).

The practice of communicating with the shareholders on a public company's share register is a discipline in its own right. In the UK, the flotations of the former building societies and their transformation into public companies along with newly privatised companies such as BT and British Gas plc created companies with large numbers of shareholders. When the Halifax Building Society floated in June 1997, between spring 1996 and June 1997 it sent out 65 million separate communications. On its first day of trading 7.6 million people owned shares worth £18 billion (Pugh, 1998). Communicating with such large numbers of shareholders required specialist skills opening up a new phase of financial communication, one that has developed its own skill set and practitioners.

Originally IR was carried out by a financial PR company and/or a merchant bank advising the firm. While many firms continue to provide this service, nowadays most investor relations departments, especially at large quoted companies, tend to be in-house. Significantly, when undertaken in-house IR is, separated from the communications/PR department. Marston and Straker's (2001) research demonstrated that the company senior executive in charge can be the chief executive but more usually is the finance director. This enables direct communication to be undertaken with a company's key financial audiences through, for example, roadshows or one-to-one communication with shareholders. Communication is also carried out electronically through the company website, webinars, webcasts and conference calls. Marston's (1996) research into the preferred communication of sell-side analysts found that direct telephone calls from the company and preferably from the finance director and/or chief executive were the most important followed by (in order of importance) telephone conference calls, roadshows, internet conferences, investor relations releases received by fax, quarterly reports, plant and site visits and divisional presentations.

Stock market analysts are employed by financial institutions to advise retail and institutional clients on whether they should buy or sell a company's shares. As they key influencers on a public company's share price, Arvidsson (2012: 109) found that the communication between public companies and financial analysts has increased in the last 15 years and continues to grow: "The prime incentive for engaging in communication is to teach financial analysts (and the market) about the company." While both the company and analysts prefer 'direct contact' as a means of communication, this presents problems for the management involved as it, "risks directing away the management's focus from other important management tasks" (Arvidsson 2012: 109).

The importance of investor relations is highlighted by Argawal et al. (2015: 35). "The IR industry argues that a company's investment in IR activity raises its profile with market participants leading to enhanced firm value." The purpose of their research "is to test the value of IR programmes" (2015: 35). Their research finds that when constructing their optimal portfolios – investors only use the securities they know about.

> If investment in IR activity serves to raise a firm's profile with market participants, then we predict that the firm value will be greater. However, if firms are already well known and followed then investment in IR may have little incremental value and could lead to firm valuation if costs are significant.

The modern financial PR consultancy

Staff of financial PR consultancies in the 1970s and 1980s were largely ex-journalists as the primary purpose of the consultancy was gaining media coverage for their clients.

The modern financial PR consultancy, however, is a more sophisticated organisation, offering a wider range of services reflecting both the global ambitions and reach of their clients. Servicing them demands a different skill set from the financial PR companies discussed above; the changing employment patterns was highlighted in Butterick's (2015) research. While a journalism background remains the largest single category at the 12 leading financial PR firms (19%), a background in investment/merchant banking is increasing (11%).

Having ex- financial journalists working for the consultancy has an advantage for the media.

> Understanding what we are looking for is very important. Financial PRs from a similar background to our own know our approach and send us relevant and appropriate material, they have to understand how we might treat the story and what we can or cannot do

said one business editor. "While claiming that having a background in financial media does not necessarily mean that PR practitioners have any special privileges, it clearly makes a difference if you are approached by an ex-colleague with a story."

> Financial journalism is such a specialised area; all the London-based journalists for example know each other where they came from. Even if you are working on a rival newspaper you might spend more time on a story with colleagues from rival news organisations. So if someone you know contacts you about a story then, yeah you are going to look at that before you look at what someone you don't know says.
>
> (Butterick, 2015: 118).

One significant recent trend has been the merger between financial PR and public affair companies creating companies with international connections and offering providing a global service for their clients.

There has been an increasing synergy between financial PR and public affairs companies, either through mergers or with financial PR firms opening their own subsidiaries. A combined service offers clients a capacity to influence business media and legislation. Lobbying can be a legitimate part of the political process, if, for example, a government is planning to introduce legislation affecting a particular industry then it is legitimate to ascertain the views of the industry on how it might be affected. Simply defined lobbying is when an individual or group tries to persuade a government minister or department to support a specific policy or campaign. The term originates from the lobby of the House of Commons where a constituent could meet their MP.

Global growth has either been achieved by opening their own international offices or through a merger with another company that, in addition to global reach, also has complementary services. What was the UK's largest financial PR company, Financial Dynamics, was brought in 2009 by FTI Consulting and now categorises itself as a multi-agency management consultancy. FTI Consulting topped the global table in terms of deal volume, working on 94 deals worth US$44 billion. In 2024 the firm was an adviser to 48 of the FTSE 100 companies and claims to have over 8,000 experts in 33 countries, territories and 87 cities around the globe (www.fticonsulting.co.uk).

The danger to society that lobbying poses can be demonstrated by the energy sector where groups on both sides of the climate issue have powerful campaigns designed to influence government policy. Activist groups such as Greenpeace and Friends of the Earth are sophisticated lobbyists for their cause. They cannot match however the financial and political power of the energy lobby where they have attempted to limit legislation that they believe might adversely affect their sector. Is it right that they should have such power to influence legislation that impacts on the future of the planet?

Financial calendar work

The increased financial PR and investor relations activity by public companies has been driven by legislation introduced by successive governments as society demands increasing transparency from public companies.

The financial communications work of a public company is dominated by the demands of the financial calendar where there are two key dates when a public company must release its results to the outside world – at six months (the interims) and the year end (the finals). All public companies have to follow the basic legal rule that any information that might impact on its share price has to be made available to everyone at the same time. Authorship of the announcement press release is a combined affair and will include not only identified authors such as the internal PR department but also, the company finance director, and the legal department. External advisers such as the merchant bank, stockbroker, financial PR, IR, corporate lawyers may also be asked to comment. The release is then issued to the external world through RNS, the Stock Exchange's own distribution network to the media and available on the company website. While the main PR function appears to be concentrated on results day, in fact in many cases it will probably have started well before the results are issued. Off the record briefings may have been offered to key journalists to explain and contextualise the forthcoming results; this can be quite a difficult job because no information must be imparted in any way to indicate what the results might be.

Traditionally results day used to be a carefully choreographed and managed affair; the company finance director and chief executive would go through a series of meetings with analysts and their institutional investors to explain the results. Based on the results and the comments from the FD and CEO the analysts will then either recommend clients buy or sell the company shares and this can impact on the share price. Analysts would prefer individual meetings, but in practice they are usually held with other analysts and nowadays electronically through either teams or zoom.

Some key journalists might be invited to the analyst briefing and individual interviews with key publications will also be carried out. Online news sites are making a big difference to the communication process, since news about the company results and the reaction during the day – whether, for example, the share price has gone up or down – are reported in real time.

Two other parts of the financial calendar involving the PR function are the Annual General Meeting and production and distribution of the Annual Report. The Annual General Meeting is a big, set-piece affair to which all shareholders are invited to attend and comment on the year's figures and the performance of the executive management.

The digital age is however impacting on this as well with increasing demands to end costly in-person AGMs and move to online conferences. The argument for their retention is that the AGM remains an opportunity for small investors to directly address the chairman, something they are rarely able to do. The board of Barclays bank, for example, were subject to two hours of small shareholder fury at a packed Royal Festival Hall in 2014 over director bonuses.

Most AGMs however are not like that, few shareholders turn up to them and the outcome of resolutions are usually agreed in advance by the large financial institutions and the board. Questions at the AGM are increasingly vetted in advance. "As a means of effective communication between companies and shareholders, annual meetings are losing their purpose" (Pratley, 2023: 32). According to the 1985 Companies Act, the quorum for a general meeting is two. Archie Norman, chair of M&S and a veteran of other boards is part of a campaign to allow online AGMs that were permitted during the pandemic.

M&S reported that three times as many people attended a digital event in 2020 as attended its physical event in 2019.

The Annual Report is another statutory document that used to be at the heart of the public company financial communication. It summarises what the company has done in the past year and what its plans are for the next year. In the 1980s and 1990s they were lavish productions costing thousands to produce. Currently however, mindful of new trends and responsibilities, companies increasing refer to the Environmental, Social and Governance (ESG) performance as well as the financial.

Note

1 There were very few women working in the City at senior levels; their role was confined to support ones such as typists and secretaries.

3 Paradigms, worldviews and ideology

Financial public relations (PR) is a specialist area of PR and to understand the theoretical issues associated with it we must first identify how it relates to the theoretical debates in PR. In PR the Excellence/Symmetrical paradigm is the dominant paradigm developed initially by Grunig and Hunt (1984). It remains the main reference point in theoretical debates and the benchmark against which other theories are debated. Botan and Taylor (2004) were the first to identify Excellence Theory as the dominant PR paradigm which[1] developed from research among PR practitioners in the US and the UK. Its purpose was to discover what made excellent PR practice and what PR practitioners should do to follow it.

In financial communications Alexander Laskin's theory and definition of investor relations (IR) is based on his historical interpretation on how it has developed and has become the dominant paradigm (Lakskin, 2010).

An important issue in this debate is how and why do paradigms become dominant in their fields? Are they immutable and unchanging or, do they change according to different circumstances? It is my contention that if financial PR is to have any future relevance, then it must have a new paradigm, one not uncritically based on a market knows best philosophy. It should be a paradigm that embraces not only the belief that a company has to work for all its stakeholders but that it has a wider responsibility to issues such as global warming.

According to Kuhn (1962), the dominant paradigm is,

> the most popular or majority approach to the subject. The dominant paradigm in a field comprises the framework and methodologies that guide most research in the field and which are regarded as the most important ideas. Ultimately these ideas become ingrained into a set of formal beliefs about what the discipline stands for. The dominant paradigm is supported by sets of assumptions or taken for granted beliefs, which may lead to blinkered thinking.

The paradigms in PR and financial PR

On a personal level a paradigm might best be described as a mental filter through which we view the world and make meaning or sense of our life

DOI: 10.4324/9780429323584-3

experiences. The mental filters are defined by a constellation of personal core beliefs that influence our everyday decisions. A personal paradigm allows us to think, perceive and even act without having to process and absorb new everyday experiences.

L'Etang (2008: 10) offers the following definition of a paradigm it is,

A worldview that frames and influences our approach to everything we see...it comprises taken-for-granted values, assumptions and approaches to the world. A paradigm in the academic context will be apparent by references to the same names or concepts which will be presented as basic knowledge of a field, that does not require to be explained in detail each time or defended.

Barnes (1982: 11/17) highlights how a paradigm becomes established in academia. As presented in a textbook a paradigm is an: "Existing scientific achievement, a specific concrete problem, solution which has gained universal acceptance throughout a scientific field as a valid procedure and a model of valid procedure for pedagogic use." Examples from science include Carnot's Cycle, Mendel's experimental work on 'inheritance in peas,' Bohr on the electronic orbits of the hydrogen, and Crick and Watson on DNA.

The theory becomes established through several well-trodden routes, such as, the author speaking at conferences, writing textbooks and contributing to academic journals, they all play their role in helping to establish the paradigm. L'Etang (2008: 11) explains the importance of the textbook in transmitting the dominant paradigm: "A textbook serves as a medium through which the direction of development in a field is reaffirmed and also functions as a mechanism for self-perpetuation." Arguably, Laskin's 2018 *Handbook of Financial Communications and Investor Relations* is a textbook example of this.

Through the textbook and coursework students come across the paradigm; and it then defines their training and practice routines.

In this way the structures of paradigms are thoroughly assimilated and the procedures involved are mastered and become routine accomplishments. The culture of an established natural science is passed on in the form of paradigms. The central task of the teacher is to display them. The central task of the student is to assimilate them and to acquire competence in their routine use. The most satisfactory way of describing scientific knowledge is simply as a repertoire of paradigms.

(Barnes, 1982: 17)

Once a paradigm is established it shapes debates about the nature of the discipline since potential alternative paradigms define themselves in relation to it. Other than the lack of a research based alternative, a number of reasons have been suggested for Excellence Theory's dominance. Excellence Theory improves and enhances the reputation of PR and can be read as a 'bad-to-good typology' (Moloney, 2006: 142) distancing PR today from the bad old days of press agentry and propaganda to where it now functions at a level that adds value to society. It also advances the discipline and helps to provide an image of PR that is flattering and self-serving and is therefore popular with pro-PR voices: "In offering an evaluative scale, the paradigm has allowed judgment about the practice of PR... it has made PR respectable. It has made it teachable at public expense" (Moloney, 2006: 86). In a discipline struggling with questions of ethics and professional status, this is important.

Huang and Lu (2012: 60) identify how citations of the key publications in the Excellence study have increased since 2002 demonstrating its dominance of theoretical debate in PR, "It essentially means that excellence study remains an important part of the public relations literature." Its geographic impact has also spread from outside the English-speaking world.[2] "Excellence study, a theory developed out of a western cultural context, has influenced higher education in at least 16 countries." (2012: 60) As further evidence of its impact it is also cited across a wide range of disciplines, not just PR but advertising, business, economics and communications are major disciplines routinely citing Excellence study. Its international impact is illustrated by Excellence Theory being cited in 385 non-English works in 24 languages over the last 20 years.

The Excellence research was based on the work of PR practitioners and identified four models of PR practice, press agentry/publicity model, the public information model, two-way asymmetrical communication and two-way symmetrical model.

In practice, PR practitioners utilise different methods according to the type of work they are undertaking; the fourth model however, remains the ideal standard to which all PR practitioners should aspire to. Practising it, so it is argued produces excellent PR. The key feature is that the company or organisation carries out symmetrical communication with stakeholders; essential to the theory is that all stakeholders are equal and none has or enjoys better privileges in terms of passing information than the other. Symmetrical communication believes that the organisation not only disseminates information to stakeholders but also receives feedback from them. The crucial point about this dialogue between the organisation and its stakeholders is that the organisation is prepared to change its policy as a result it. Grunig and Hunt (1984: 23) state that: "The two-way symmetric model...consists more of a dialogue than a monologue. Symmetrical communication takes place through dialogue, negotiation, listening, and conflict management rather than through persuasion, manipulation, and the giving of orders."

Grunig (2009) prefers the term 'World View' for "the way in which people make sense of the world and understand what it right and wrong, is a primary reason for why people think and behave as they do..." For Grunig, 'paradigm' as developed in the philosophy of science by Thomas Kuhn, is the scientific equivalent of world view, the problem though for paradigms is that they change and develop:

> Some philosophers such as Collingwood (1940), Kuhn (1970), Feyerabend (1970) and Bohm (1977) have argued that world views are completely subjective. They believed that people, groups, societies choose one world view rather than another by arguing, fighting, voting or mobilising supporters – a dialectical process – rather than through reason, negotiation, or compromise.
>
> (Grunig, 2009: 72)

Dominant paradigms, however, are not meant to last forever. They are imperfect:

> In agreeing upon a paradigm, scientists do not accept a finished product: rather, they agree to accept it as a basis for future work and to treat as illusory or eliminable all its apparent inadequacies and defects. Paradigms are refined and elaborated in normal science. And they are used in the development of further problem–solutions, thus extending the scope of scientific competencies and procedures.
>
> (Grunig, 2009: 46)

Science evolves through paradigm change the current dominant paradigm becomes 'normal' science,' satisfactorily explaining the world, for a time no limit is put on the timescale of its dominance. New discoveries, new ways of looking at the world, come along and disrupt the ruling paradigm and for a time the new and old paradigms compete; while the proponents of the two paradigms speak the same language they see the world in completely different ways. Kuhn (1962) describes this as incommensurability. Eventually, the new paradigm replaces the old paradigm. As new ideas and circumstances emerge and as capitalism itself struggles for an identity on how to redefine itself in the face of environmental challenges, so financial communications will need a new paradigm to encompass these changes.

Grunig however implies that World Views exist and continue for ever and ever: "The world view of the two-way symmetrical model has been articulated throughout history and especially in the history of public relations."

Financial PR paradigm

Laskin's IR theory (2010, 2018) has become the accepted paradigm in financial communications by following the course outlined above – writing books and journal papers, speaking at conferences, and editing an influential textbook. How this works in practice can be illustrated by Doan and McKie (2017) in their literature review of IR. David McKie is an established and respected writer on PR and a leading Critical PR theorist. He is though, not though an expert on financial PR relying on other sources for the history of its development. Unsurprisingly because of no alternatives, Doan & McKie uncritically accept Laskin's historical background of IR on which his theory is based, Laskin's (2010) research divides IR practice into three phases: Communication (1945–1970), finance (1970–2000) and synergy (early 2000s now).

> In the first phase, IR started out as an extension of PR and was limited to publicity and tactical work, which did not meet the increasing information demands of financial publics. The failure of these early professionals prompted organisations to separate IR from PR and focus on financial data in the next phase. In this second phase, the goal was to maximise share price through building relationships with institutional investors. Since 2000 (following corporate scandals such as the collapse of Enron and Worldcom) IR has entered the third phase, the phase of synergy, where communication and finance professionals work together to improve understanding and create a fair valuation of the company.
>
> (2010: 2)

By accepting Laskin's arguments Doan & McKie are identifying Laskin as the authority figure and contribute to establishing his argument as the dominant paradigm in financial communications.

Dolphin (2004) noted the lack of research around IR, quoting Farraghe et al. (1994) who suggest that academic journals have largely ignored the topic. In such a vacuum it becomes easier to build a paradigm that appears to be credible.

To be fair to Laskin, he is one of the few academic authors who has taken financial communication and IR seriously and his scholarship and research has enhanced its credibility. However, one of the problems with his history of financial PR is that, as we saw in Chapter 2, the history and development of financial communications in the UK took a different route than in the USA and it is hard to see how the theory can be claimed to be universally applicable.

Laskin, though, has a different goal than just establishing a dominant paradigm in the sector, and that is to use financial communications to 'prove' that Grunig's Excellence/symmetrical theory works in practice. If Laskin does this, then he will overcome a key criticism of Excellence Theory that it has no practical application.

Laskin (Kelly et al., 2010: 182) claims his research, "is the first to find the predominant practice of the normative model." It refutes:

> Long-standing criticism that the symmetrical model is a utopian model. The two-way symmetrical model does exist in the real world, and it can be found in the bastion of capitalism – publicly owned corporations in the United States.

Symmetrical communication in investor relations

Laskin (2010) argues that IR is "one of the most important functions of modern corporations" and in his version it become not just a financial practice but one with an economic significance which impacts on the whole economy:

> Investor Relations is responsible for raising shareholder capital to enable corporations to implement their vision into reality. Investor relations help companies survive through various stages by enabling access to shareholder capital. Finally, investor relations ensures corporate executives are doing everything they can to lead corporations to long-term sustainable growth, while simultaneously benefiting society and providing financial returns to shareholders.
>
> (2010: 1)

This argument should be seen as the latest stage in the debate that PR should be situated at the most senior levels of company management. According to PR theorists, when the finance director manages IR it will be limited in its function but when controlled by PR it offers important strategic advice to the company. For the finance sector the discussions are around operational efficiency, however, for the PR sector it is a more existential argument, a chance to demonstrate its seriousness and impact.

The 'finance side' of the company, however, have a completely different interpretation on the role of financial PR; after interviewing finance directors from UK public companies Arfin (1994: 39) dismisses the claims that anyone from a PR background could offer a company strategic advice. "They (financial PR practitioners) simply don't have the skills," said one, "and no matter how well they think they know us, we know our own business better." "When you've got a financial PR who thinks he's some kind of business strategist, then you've got trouble," said another.

> If a strategic approach develops out of a communications tactic, the general feeling seems to be that it is a stroke of serendipity and nothing more. None of the companies visited would expect to obtain this kind of help from a financial public or investor relations consultant.

Laskin (2010), argues that IR has a wider impact. The responsibility of the IR Officer is to "make sure the interests of investors and shareholders are taken into account" by the company.

In this role they are practising symmetrical communications, not only sending information on behalf of the company out to shareholders, but also representing the views of the shareholder to the company board and, significantly, perhaps encouraging the board to change its policy because of this interaction.

Laskin argues that symmetrical communication enables the voices of the shareholders to be heard in the boardroom. Significantly though this ignores evidence about the changing nature of shareholders.

> Previously, (in the earlier phases) investor relations was often equated with disclosure – we put information out there, the rest is not our business. The shareholders, however, demanded to be heard. The feedback loop in communications is a necessity. As the influence of shareholders grows, the companies that refuse to listen to shareholders suffer.
>
> (Laskin, 2010: 11)

No company has one coherent body of 'shareholders' but several groups with different interests in a company. With the GameStop for example (see Chapter 4), there were two groups of shareholders with completely different visions for the company. There are numerous examples of where the voices of retail shareholders have put demands to the company management limiting executive pay and the environment, for instance and the large institutional shareholders acting in conjunction with the management have defeated often critical voices. Then there are so-called 'activist' institutional shareholders who take a position in a company that they regard as undervalued to try and change the management. Who in these situations will the financial PR/IR consultant represent?

The shareholders or the Executive Management and where differences exist should it be the function of financial PR practitioner to reconcile them?

Ideology and public relations

Destutt de Tracy first used 'Ideology' in 1796 when looking to create 'a new science of ideas, an idea-logy, which would be the ground of all other sciences' (McLellan, 1986: 6). As a materialist he believed that the ideas we have are not given to us by God or nature but are the result of the interaction between our physical sciences and our external environment. "A rational investigation of the origins of ideas, free from religious or metaphysical prejudice would be the foundation of a just and happy society" (McLellan, 1986: 6). Ideology, according to this view, is the study of how ideas are created based on experience.

According to Richardson (2007), ideology "is not just any system of ideas or beliefs but ways of thinking in which historically transient forms of social organisations are represented as eternal, natural, inevitable or 'rational'".

Kersten (1994: 113) argues that:

> Ideology, simply defined, is a particular world view that serves to support and protect existing power relations. Ideologies are world views in that they make people recognize...1) what exists and what does not exist, 2)

what is good, right, just, beautiful, attractive, enjoyable and its opposites, 3) what is possible and impossible…etc. By specifying what is real, desirable and possible, ideology shapes our consciousness, creating a particular rendition of reality and excluding others. What makes a world view ideological, however, is not that it provides a certain socially constructed reality. Rather, it is the way in which this reality functions in relation to existing power structures that makes it ideological.

PR theorists however, do not like the idea of ideology because it is an essential element of the media superstructure where ideological battle rages. The media in society can be regarded as an ideological formation reflecting the class struggle and "constitute simultaneously and contradictorily the site and the ideological conditions of the transformation of the relations of production" (Pecheux, Quoted in Butterick, 2015: 142).

"The primary impact of ideology, therefore, is in the formation and transformation of human subjectivity in the way in which it operates to create not merely a certain point of view, but a way of existing, a way of being-in-the world." (Kersten, 1994: 114).

In one of the few PR academic papers to discuss ideology, Nneka Logan (2014) explores what she rightly describes as "the under-theorized relationship between ideology and public relations."

As Logan recognises, ideology does not just have one definition or association. "Ideologies, however, are not always inextricably linked to some form of exploitation and do always have to be bad or negative. Ideologies can exist on a continuum." (2014: 663). It can and should be used as critical tool to identify ideologies within an idea.

If we want to use ideology to understand ideas, then analysing how language is used becomes essential to this. Critical stylist Leslie Jeffries (2010), for example, believes that an 'ideology' exits in every text and argues we can use critical analytical tools to understand and identify the ideology in a text:

> Unlike its use in the popular press and some political environments, we do not use the term ideology to refer only to terms that are motivated by political aims or selfish intentions. That is not to say that all ideology is equal; clearly some ideology is potentially harmful, some may be a force for good, and some is simply culturally restricted or a question of choice. The important issue is that language can carry ideologies, either explicitly (I hate foreigners) or implicitly (those horrible foreigners are back again). It is common, but often implicit in analytical contexts, to take for granted that we are most interested in the less obvious ideological encoding, because it is more insidious.

We can identify here a link between paradigms and ideology in the way they shape and influence perception. The ideological content in some texts may be open and clear to all…when it is: "repeated endlessly in so many different forms in all sorts of texts, to the point where it becomes naturalised as self-evident or common sense" (Jeffries, 2010).

While Excellence Theory has given PR a better image, the reality is that it is largely uncritical of corporate and social excesses and still serves as a servant of a form of capitalism that produces gross inequalities of wealth and environmental damage.

Despite this sensitivity around its ideological associations, Laskin (2010) directly equates his definition of IR practice with an ideology, the Efficient Market Hypothesis (EFM). As EFM plays an important role in maintaining the hegemony of 'the market,' this sustains the argument of critics that PR is defender of capitalism and the status quo.

Laskin (2010: 11) argues the 'earlier goal' of IR activity was: "to have a positive effect on the share price – the higher the better…" citing Enron[3] as an example of what happens when this policy is pursued. According to his history however, the market and the consideration of the share price has moved on since then and both investors and public company are now agreed on, 'fair value' for the share price as opposed to 'high value.'

Pursuing fair value also helps IR to become, "integrated into the top management decisions process, based on two-way communications, and aiming for a fair stock valuation – can become a source of competitive advantage for a corporation…" (2010: 11).

Under the Laskin model all relevant information about a company and its performance is publicly available and crucially participants in share buying and selling have equal access to this information at the same time. According to the theory all investors are rational and capable of evaluating the information available to them again on equal terms. "IR is charged with providing the information from the company to shareholders, financial analysts and other market participants…"

Ensuring that all relevant information is available to market participants is not only important to the company Laskin believes but the wider economy. "The survival of modern capitalism depends on how well IRs perform their task in ensuring equal access to information for various market participants…" (2010: 11). IR must ensure that they key assumptions of the Efficient Market Hypothesis is met through extensive and timely disclosure of all relevant info about the company and its stock.

Significantly there is no criticism of market capitalism and its role in creating myriad social and environmental issues. This places financial communication as an important servant of market capitalism and helps sustain the argument that the market has the answers to all economic issues. The ideological basis of Laskin's work is to assert the primacy of the market at a time when market-based solutions alone appear to be the cause of environmental problems and not the solution. To play its part in a transformation, financial PR will need to work with a new paradigm that provides an alternative vision to the market-based solutions. It is my contention that as this stage of capitalism is being challenged so financial PR must have a different model.

Notes

1 In the 1982 the management theorist Tom Peters and his colleague Bob Waterman published 'In Search of Excellence,' their study of what made companies excellent and leaders in their fields. The Excellent PR Project was a research project designed to identify what made the best PR practice.
2 Huang and Lu argue that the interest in Excellence may have grown because of increased use of the internet as a search engine and not necessarily because the theory itself is any more popular.
3 Enron collapsed in 2001 at the time it held more than $60 billion in assets. It also led to the collapse of its accountants, Arthur Andersen which at the time was one of the largest accountancy firms in the world. While it might be argued that the ultimate cause of Enron's collapse was down to the pursuit of a higher share price but the immediate cause was a series of accounting scandals.

4   Shareholders and the public company

Laskin believes it is the role of investor relations (IR) to identify potential shareholders; and the future of capitalism depends on IR achieving this; while this has no doubt assisted his credibility and reputation with the IR industry it must be questioned whether this is an accurate reflection of reality. We need to consider in more detail what a shareholder is and how it fits into the corporate structure.

The idea that 'shareholders' are an unchanging, homogenous group – as regularly implied by the media and politicians – is incorrect but rarely reflected in the literature. The balance for example, between the numbers of retail and institutional shareholders constantly changes, as does the composition of the institutional shareholders. This has implications for the way financial communications is undertaken. Currently there are more institutional than retail investors but this was not always the case, it is only relatively recently that private individuals owned most of the shares.

Shares in public companies can be bought and sold by anyone. The share owner becomes a shareholder and, along with all the other shareholders, the owner of the company. In doing so they are participating in one of the most enduring but controversial company structures in economic history.

The public company is a remarkable entity: from its joint-stock forerunner in the 17th century to the modern version, it has adapted to changing economic and social situations, surviving major conflicts and ideological battles. Currently it faces another existential threat as critics point to its role and responsibility in the ecological crisis threatening the planet and there are many who doubt whether in its current structure it has the capacity to change.

Public companies are typically the largest and most influential businesses in the economy of a country and their actions impact on the rest of society. Public companies can shape an economy, the strategies they pursue has a wide-ranging impact. As they are for example, usually among the largest employers in the country, they contribute significant revenues to the economy through taxes, either in terms of the direct tax paid or through the taxes paid by their employees.

DOI: 10.4324/9780429323584-4

To its supporters the public company has been the engine of sustained economic growth, enabling capitalist economies to dominate economically and create wealth for millions. As evidence of its strength, supporters point to the way that former state-controlled economies in China and Russia have adopted their own version of the public company and re-structured their economies along market orientated lines.

To its critics the public company has created huge disparities in wealth, the amassed power and wealth of individual corporations is greater than that of many countries but unfortunately is used to satisfy the needs of a small minority at the expense of the majority.

There is nothing new about criticisms of the public company; it has been viewed with suspicion throughout its history. Following the scandal of the South Sea Bubble in 1720, Adam Smith, the apostle of the free market believed that joint-stock companies should be established only under rare circumstances. The managers were, he argued, "rather of other people's money than of their own, it cannot well be expected that they should watch over with the same anxious vigilance with which the partners in a private company frequently watch over their own." (Smith, A. Quoted in Butterick, 2015). This relationship between the owners, the shareholders and the company managers is a recurring theme and has been a decisive factor in shaping its direction and a cause of major problems.

The form of public company we are discussing is a specific economic and cultural manifestation frequently known as the Anglo-Saxon model because it dominates the USA/UK economies (although there are differences between the two countries in the amount of regulation covering them). The Anglo-Saxon model is associated with a Board of Directors and shareholders. Managers derive their authority from the board, based on shareholders' approval. There are, however, different models of public companies, the so-called German and European model is managed by two groups, a supervisory council and an executive board.

Private companies are closed companies, where share ownership is in the hands of the company owner, their family and friends these shares are not usually available for purchase by the public. With public companies any individual can buy or sell shares through an increasingly diverse range of sources. The term 'public limited company' was introduced in the UK in 1983 to differentiate between the private limited company and the public company whose shares are quoted on the London Stock Exchange.

The essential characteristic of public companies is that their shareholders own them; to qualify as a shareholder you must own at least one share[1] of a company's issued share capital. A shareholder (or stockholder) can be an individual, company or financial institution. According to Sheridan and Kendall (1992) the UK position on corporate governance is based on the premise that a company is a piece of property, a right that is limited by the extent of their shareholding, hence the term, limited liability.

Share owners, whether owning one share or 1 million, own them because they want a financial return on their investment. All share owners receive the same payment, a dividend payment paid twice a year when the company makes a profit. They can also sell their shares hopefully for more than they paid for them[2].

In a public company there is a separation between the owners (the shareholders) and the executive managers who are appointed by the shareholders to run the business on their behalf. Adam Smith thought that in almost all circumstances the private company was a superior form of organisation because the managers were involved in the business as its owners. The question of how to make the managers of public companies have the same degree of involvement and motivation as the shareholders has been a key issue that has shaped public company structure. It has had wider economic significance through the ideology used to justify shareholder dominance.

At its core is agency theory (Jensen and Meckling, 1976) which argues that the executive management of the company are the agents of the shareholders and run the business on their behalf. The agent (the executive management) represents the principal (shareholders) in a business transaction. In a private company, in contrast, the executives who run it are usually also the only shareholders so management and owners are the same. The agent is then expected to represent the best interests of the principal without regard to their own self-interest.

Debt, equity finance and shareholders

Before considering the changing nature of shareholdings it is necessary to understand where equity finance fits into business finance.

In business finance a distinction is made between debt and equity finance. Debt finance is a form of finance conventionally provided by banks and includes, for example, loans and credit finance. Equity finance is raised by a company selling their shares to external parties, equity shareholders, are also known as ordinary shareholders. Debt finance is usually short-term, conventional bank loans, for example, are term loans usually of five to ten years. Equity finance in contrast is meant to be long-term finance where the company has no obligation to repay the investors. Shareholders can exit the company either through selling their shares to other shareholders, back to the company or third parties such as venture capital companies. Debt finance is repaid through regular loan repayments and takes money out of the business, which can have an impact on a company's cash-flow. Equity owners are paid dividends twice a year on the shares they own. Debt finance repayments must be paid irrespective of whether a company makes a profit or not and is usually secured either against property or shares. Overall, equity finance is regarded as a positive and beneficial form of finance, enabling companies to raise large amounts of finance where the risk is spread among several shareholders.

Changing nature of shareholders

There are two types of shareholders – retail and institutional. Retail shareholders are individuals who buy and sell shares on their own account. Gurrola-Perez et al. (2002) state that a retail investor is a: "concept (that) broadly refers to an individual trading in a personal account for his/her own benefit." And while some of the world's stock exchanges require a legal definition, overall there is no, "homogenous definition of a retail investor across markets" (Gurrola-Perez et al., 2002).

Institutional shareholders are traditionally financial institutions such as pension funds, insurance companies, life assurance companies, unit and investment trusts. Hedge funds are more recent entrants, and their investment timescale tends to be more short-term which can have serious implications for the companies they invest in. Any profit a company makes are distributed on a range of activities such as investment in new projects and machinery or taking over a company.

While these activities are important they are not the principle priority of a public company which is to make dividend payments to the owners, its shareholders. Controversially, some companies attempt to maintain their dividend payments even when profits are falling. This is because not making a dividend payment to shareholders is regarded as a serious failure by the executive management, suggesting their strategy has failed. The consequences of this for the Chief Executive responsible for formulating the strategy can be severe and could lead to their dismissal.

Dividend payments are made twice a year after the company has announced its interim (six month) and final (year-end) results (although there are some companies that make an annual payment). The original rationale for making two payments was to spread shareholders income more evenly. For both retail and institutional shareholders, these regular dividend payments on their shares provide an important income. This was the reason, why for example the Bronte sisters were keen investors in railway shares. In 1849 when their railway shares fell to their lowest point a rueful Charlotte Bronte wrote,

> My shares are in the York and North Midland Railway. The original price of the shares in the company was £50. At one time they rose to £120; and for years they gave a dividend of 10% they are now down to £20 and it is doubtful whether any dividend will be paid this year....
>
> (Quoted in Butterick, 2015)

Pension funds and insurance companies traditionally invested in equities to provide them with a regular income to meet pay-outs for insurance and pension claims.

Increasingly, many public companies are using their profit to buy shares back from shareholders. This is controversial because it restricts the total number of shares in circulation and increases the power of the executive management who organised the share buyback. The justification for it is that the shareholders benefit as the buyback offers them a higher price than the prevailing market price.

From the 1960s direct investments in public company shares in the USA and UK by the traditional financial investors began to fall. Pension funds, unit trusts, insurance companies, developed alternative investment vehicles aimed at consumers enabling investors to invest indirectly in public companies more safely. There has also been a decline in share ownership by retail investors. In 1963 over 50% of UK shares were owned by individual investors in 2020 (ONS) retail investors owned just 12% of UK quoted shares. Interestingly, there has been a rise since the 2008 low-point of 10.2%.

While noting the differences between retail and institutional shareholders, Gurrola-Perez et al. (2002: 34) argue that both bring something different to a company:

> In general, domestic institutional investors provide stability (to a company) because they hold shares for the long-term and trade in larger amounts. Retail participants bring liquidity: they tend, however, to be volatile (investors) and more responsive to liquidity or volatility shocks.

The decline in retail investing has been a consistent trend throughout all the world's stock exchanges. However, the 2020 Covid pandemic, when people were forced to stay home, appears to have resulted in an increase in trading. Another factor helping driving this increase was the emergence of new technology, share trading through mobile phone apps. "The pandemic spurred investment activity…long periods of time at home during the pandemic, ease of opening accounts and the ability to invest small amounts facilitated mostly smaller trades" (BNY Mellon, 2022: 13).

Gurrola-Perez et al. (2002: 28) confirm the positive impact that the pandemic had on share trading by retail investors. There was:

> a significant impact on the levels of retail participation in many markets. Around 65% of exchanges in the survey reported an increase in retail participation during the first months of the Covid-19 pandemic, against 24% who did not observe any change.

This helped drive significant increases in market activity when institutional investments fell – a 26% year on year increase in the US and in Canada a 64% increase in monthly trading volumes in March 2020 (for the same month the previous year it was 6%).

Among the factors identified by the various stock exchanges for this increase were changing macroeconomic conditions; new technologies making markets easier to access; user-friendly interfaces of mobile apps, and the influence of social media. Significantly, this increase in share buying and selling has continued to grow in some markets since the pandemic ended. The US Federal Reserve demonstrated that 41% of the total financial assets of US households and non-profits had direct and indirect holdings of stocks in December 2021, the highest figure since 1952. According to the Investment Company Institute, 50% of US adults own stocks, 80% of high-income earners own stocks (earning over $70,000), 50% of middle earners and 20% of low-income families (earning less than $30,000 per annum).

Share buying and selling has always had moral critics with some regarding it as little more than another form of gambling, an opportunity to make a 'killing' to quickly transform the lives of participants. As history demonstrates new and inexperienced investors remain vulnerable to the hype around so-called 'bubbles' where share prices rise quickly and there appears to be an opportunity to make a profit quickly.

An issue here is the recurring question of where investors get information from to help them make their investment decisions. A 2022 BNY Mellon survey provides an interesting insight into where modern investors source their information. The research divided investors into four categories, nascent investors, traditional investors, established investors and retirement investors. Nascent investors are the youngest and least experienced investors and 57% of them trade shares using their mobile phones.

Information to help their investment decisions came from a diverse range of sources: 17% used analysts' reports, 14% online news, 12% access social media for decisions, 11% company websites, while 8% only relied on traditional media. An indication of the changing communication pattern.

Share bubbles also provide a fascinating insight into the psychology of investing and investors. History demonstrates they have five stages: displacement, boom, euphoria, profit-taking and bust. While their time-frames vary, each stage typically only lasts a few weeks or at most a few months they always have the same characteristics: rapidly increasing share prices which eventually reach an unsustainable point which then causes the share price to burst

The first recorded share bubble – and the origin of the term 'bubble' – was the South Sea Bubble of 1720. The British Government promised a monopoly to the South Sea Company (a joint-stock company) on trade with Spain's South American colonies, in exchange for taking on Britain's national debt. The South Sea Company shares soared by more than 800% over the summer of 1720, based on false rumours about the company's success. Thousands of overextended investors in every section of British society were ruined when the share price collapsed with Dukes and Duchesses to their chambermaids.

From the 17th century information from the company to current and potential owners of shares has been an integral and essential part of the buying and selling process. Throughout history, the technology of the day has been used and adapted for communication purposes. As we saw in earlier chapters, share buying and selling depends on participants receiving information about a company and the factors that might affect it as quickly as possible. Just as the internet has transformed the way in which information is distributed and accessed in every area of modern life, it is also impacting on the way shares are bought and sold and the way that public companies communicate with their target audiences. Internet-based platforms such as Instagram, YouTube and Twitter, enable investors to communicate not only with the company but also and, perhaps more significantly, with other investors and at speed.

GameStop

In January 2021, the events surrounding the US company GameStop plc brought together all elements of the new trading conditions. Some claimed at the time that what was unfolding was an investor revolution that would transform the nature of investing and put the retail investor back in control.

In 2021 GameStop was a company in apparent decline. Formerly a market leader in the USA, its stores sold video games, videos, games consoles and was the largest video and game retailer in the world. However, the growth in online retailing and streaming challenged the operation. At its height in 2006 the company once had operating profits of $600 million, which had declined to a loss of $368 million in 2021. Against the background of what appeared to be the terminal decline of the company, a number of Wall Street hedge funds started betting that the shares would go down further. The hedge fund activity was noticed by an investment group on the internet platform Reddit

Reddit, founded in 2005, claimed to be the 'front page of the internet' where people went to get all their information, rather than clicking through different sites, becoming the seventh most viewed website in the USA and eighteenth in the world. It provides users with up- to-date news, affinity groups and a place where users can create their own communities

Reddit and its community offer advice and help but does not itself recommend individual shares to buy as this type of information is regulated in the UK and USA. A subgroup of Reddit, WallStreetBets, noticed the hedge funds activity. WallStreetBets is a forum where participants discuss stock and trading options used by both experienced and inexperienced buyers and suggest trades to each other. Members were encouraged to buy GameStop shares, not to help the company, but to try and hurt the hedge funds by pushing up the share price. In the space of a week membership of the Reddit Forum tripled to 6.5 million. Their collective buying drove the share price up by 600% in just four days and meant that the Wall Street firms who had bet that the share price would go down lost billions between them. In January 2021 the GameStop share price rose 1,500% over two weeks. The share price eventually rising to a high of $347.51 and in a week GameStop market capitalisation rose from $3 billion to $25 billion. At the height of the trading frenzy 50 million shares of the company changed hands in an hour. While this might on first sight have the appearance of being another 'bubble,' there were several differences to the traditional model driven by technological developments in phone apps and services.

Mobile phone-based trading platforms allow investors to trade quickly and easily. Older brokers such as Hargreaves Lansdown have adapted to the new technology and been joined by a range of newcomers such as Freetrade, etoro and Orca, with new entrants into the market every day. E-trading software allows both institutional and retail investors to trade securities online and track share performance in real time. It is a rapidly growing industry with an estimated annual turnover of over $10 billion and over 325 operators worldwide and is expected to grow annually by 3.5%. The growth of these apps has attracted new investors who are using mobile technology they are familiar with, with the further attraction of reduced trading costs and fees for new and inexperienced investors.

RobinHood was founded in April 2013 by two former Harvard roommates Vladimir Tenev and Baiju Butt who built trading platforms for financial institutions in New York that sold trading software to hedge funds. RobinHood's popularity for users was that it was the first mobile zero-commission stock brokerage app – in other words, there was no commission to pay. It appeared in the Apple app store in December 2014 and the app was officially launched in March 2015. Before RobinHood, people used brokerage services through their laptops and computers. RobinHood was the first to be used on mobiles with a design attractive to new investors and was an instant hit with novice first-time buyers. RobinHood marketed itself as a revolutionary app with a self-declared intention to "provide everyone with access to the financial markets, not just the wealthy."

The combination of Reddit and RobinHood led some commentators to interpret the GameStop incident as an attack on traditional Wall Street firms by a new revolutionary breed of investor, a forerunner and threat to traditional ways of trading on Wall Street and similar exchanges in London and Paris. More radical supporters argued it was an attempt to democratise share trading. "Retail investors with the help of technology acting as a union is a new phenomenon. You combine the power of technology which allows you through Reddit postings to magnify your individual impact," commented Jim Paulsen, chief investment strategist at the Lenthhold Group (Li, 2021).

In reality it was nothing of the sort, as everything returned to normal after a month echoing the South Sea Bubble. This is not to say that a similar situation could not develop in the future or that there are not people wanting to challenge the trading practices of the hedge funds. The characteristic of the investors is that they believe in the system and are playing the market to make money similar to the hedge funds they claim to despise.

Perhaps the main significance of the GameStop share event, however, was the way social media influenced the share price over a short time. In the long run GameStop share price eventually fell back to its starting position, the only people making money from the trading activity were those who bought the shares at the lowest price and then sold at the higher price. As there were plenty of 'new' investors who did this, demonstrating this was less an episode of a new revolutionary anti-wall street event, than good old market capitalism. Although in this instance, unlike in the South Sea Bubble, no-one committed suicide, the activities were largely the same, with the share price manipulated by investors to their advantage on an app.

What is also interesting is that GameStop, unlike the South Sea Company, did not instigate the share price manipulation. Its press statements during the period were blandly factual simply stating what was happening, with no further comment, it was in no position to influence investor reaction. In this situation the company could do little other than issue the normal trading updates – and rising and falling share price rise had little to impact on the actual performance of the company. In contrast the South Sea Company manipulated the South Sea Bubble for its own financial benefit. In the GameStop situation, what would be the impact of the Laskin version of IR? As there were effectively two groups of shareholders warring with each other, each attempting to manipulate the situation to their own advantage. How would Laskin's vision of symmetrical communications – where the IR function feeds back to the centre the views of the investors – work? It does not of course happen like this, and in this situation the real IR function becomes apparent – to be the mouthpiece of the existing executive company management.

Gurrola-Perez et al. (2002), echo a point made by Harmsworth and Duguid that inexperienced investors need more protection, especially as they often trade because of the excitement generated by overall trading and the impact of media coverage.

The GameStop events highlighted the influence of social media in shaping retail investor behaviour and pointed to the need of enhancing investor protection. Without minimum levels of financial literacy and education, retail investors may be easily driven into misleading investment strategies. If lacking adequate protection, investors may fall victims to financial scams.

Institutional shareholders

The activity of the hedge fund investors illustrates another feature of institutional shareholders, they are becoming increasingly diverse, ONS (Office of National Statistics) figures demonstrate that since 1994 the ownership of UK public companies has been falling into foreign ownership. In 2020 56.3% of shares were owned by foreign firms, reflecting both the increasing internationalisation of the London Stock Exchange and the impact of internet trading platforms, this appears to have been encouraged by successive government's which appear to have no objection to foreign ownership of UK's companies.

In another development concerning, traditional financial institutions, which always invested in public companies for the long-term, have been dis-investing. The proportion of quoted company shares held by investment trusts fell by 0.7% points to 1.4%, the lowest since 2002. Shares held by other financial institutions based in the UK remained at 8.1%. Insurance companies' share of the market stands at 4%, falling 0.9% points from 2016 (ONS, 2023).

In addition to foreign investors, 'new equity investors,' the hedge funds, who have a shorter investment timeframe leading to what, Kay Review (2012: 10) characterises this as an, "increased fragmentation, driven by the diminishing share of large UK insurance companies and pension funds and by the globalisation of financial markers which has led to increased foreign shareholding." Significantly, this is inevitably impacting on how public companies communicate with their shareholders: "This fragmentation has reduced the incentives for engagement and the level of control enjoyed by each shareholder." The Kay Review (2012: 11) noted how long-tern investors had been replaced by:

> Asset managers – specialist investment intermediaries – have become the dominant players in the investment chain, as individual shareholding has declined, and pension funds and insurers have responded to incentives (including demographic changes and regulation) to reduce their investments in equities. Asset managers typically pay a key role in exercising the attributes of share ownership most relevant to company decision making: the right to vote and the right to buy or sell a given share.

An issue here is that by using nominee accounts it is difficult for management to identify and therefore communicate with their shareholders.

As we have noted above, technology is also changing how trading is carried out. Algorithms, for example, mean that responses to movements in share prices are made automatically and instantaneously. This encourages short-term investment; while day traders or short-sellers have always existed, modern technology is encouraging the practice:

> Some of these investors trade the market, not through the equity itself, but through synthetic derivative products including 'contracts for difference' which have been used because they do not attract stamp duty. Not only does this present a challenge for shareholder identification, it also tends to reinforce short-term movements in share prices which exacerbate market shocks.
>
> (Kay Review, 2012)

A further issue highlighted by GameStop is the speed of the news cycle and how this impacts on share trading. In today's world of instantaneous transmission of information, shocks are reported in the media on an almost real time basis and with market confidence so important in ensuring economic stability, the effect of such news becomes largely self-fulfilling.

Research for the Quoted Companies Alliance a lobby group which acts for the UK's smaller quoted companies submitted evidence to the Kay Review on whether public companies pay too much attention (or feel obliged to pay too much attention) to short-term fluctuations in their share price. "This focus on the short-term is highlighted by 41% checked their share price once daily…"

According to Kay Review (2012: 9/10)

> Overall we conclude that short-termism is a problem in UK equity markets and that the principle causes are the decline of trust and the misalignment of incentives throughout the equity investment chain. We conclude that the quality – and not the amount – of engagement by shareholders determines whether the influence of equity markets on corporate decisions is beneficial or damaging to the long-term interests of companies.

Notes

1 Companies have different types of shares, the most common, **ordinary shares**, has one vote per share and entitles the owner of the share to a dividend payment. While ordinary shares carry voting rights, they rank after preference shares with regard to capital rights.

   Non-voting ordinary shares usually carry no right to vote and no right to attend general meetings. Such shares are usually given to employees so that remuneration can be paid as dividends for the purposes of tax efficiency for both parties.

   Preference shares entitle the owner to receive a fixed amount of dividend every year. This is received ahead of individuals that hold ordinary shares. It is also usually as a percentage of the nominal value (the value stated when the shares were issued).

   Redeemable shares are issued on the terms that the company will/may buy them back at a future date. This is either fixed or, set at the director's discretion. It's usually done with non-voting shares given to employees so that if the employee leaves, the shares can be taken back at their nominal value.

2 Shares are sometimes used as security against either personal or corporate bank loans.

5　Business and ideologies

In this chapter we shall consider how Laskin's chosen ideology, the Efficient Market Theory, relates to other business philosophies and what might be the characteristics of an alternative theory. Ideologies are a form of social or political philosophy where practical and theoretical elements combine; they are a system of ideas that attempt both to explain the world and change it. Laskin deliberately associates investor relations with Efficient Market (EFM) theory an ideology that is the product of a specific phase of capitalism. Efficient Market theory is regarded as a development and improvement on Maximising Shareholder Value (MSV) which, its critics argue has contributed to creating deep unequal divisions in society and also been a major cause of the current environmental crisis.

Corporate philosophies and economic ideologies are related but neither are set in stone as they change and evolve to reflect changing economic, social and political circumstances where businesses operate. This can be demonstrated in the way economic and business philosophies have developed and changed since the end of the Second World War. We saw how financial PR evolved differently in the UK and USA, this difference is the consequence on how the two economies developed differently at the end of the Second World War.

In the UK, until 1959, capital issues and share dividends by public companies were subject to strict government control in an attempt to encourage companies to re-invest profits in their businesses with the intention of building new factories and employing people. Profit distribution was subject to a penal tax to encourage companies to plough back profits into the company rather than distribute them to shareholders. Even though such a 'socialist' philosophy was probably against the personal beliefs of many business owners and managers, the policy was nevertheless largely accepted by the UK business community. They were prepared to put the interests of the whole company before the sectional interests of any of stakeholders. This reflected the ethos of the time when, after war, society knew it had to pull together, not only to rebuild, but also try and prevent the causes of war occurring again.

DOI: 10.4324/9780429323584-5

Mass unemployment was identified as being a principle cause of war enabling fascism to develop in the inter-war period. To avoid this, post-war most western governments pursued Keynesian inspired economic policies at the heart of which was the attempt to maintain full employment. A post-war consensus developed with the main political parties pursuing a commitment to full employment.

This consensus on national economic policy lasted until the 1970s when the economic crisis caused by the oil shocks in the 1970s ended it. The changed economic situation demanded new answers to another economic problem of the 1930s, inflation. Keynesianism, according to its critics, is accused of exacerbating inflation by pumping money into the economy at a time when less money was needed in circulation. The alternative economic policy based on neoliberalism appeared to offer a solution to the problem of inflation, arguing that reducing the amount of money in circulation in the economy would lead to a fall in inflation. The theory, however, was entirely untested in practice and when put into practice it reduced inflation but only through creating mass unemployment and the destruction of key industries.

The corporate philosophy embodying the principles of neoliberalism pursued by the governments of Mrs Thatcher and President Reagan in the 1980s was Maximising Shareholder Value (MSV). Although its proponents argue it is a universal philosophy applicable to any economic situation and circumstances, this is not correct as it could only develop and thrive in a neoliberal setting. The current environmental crisis challenges the neoliberal orthodoxy and, as the theory seems outdated at a corporate level, is creating demands for new and more inclusive philosophy.

Maximising shareholder value

Maximising Shareholder Value (MSV) rose in popularity during the 1970s and was the dominant paradigm in the 1980s and 1990s and remains influential. For many years it lingered on the outer fringes of economic theory and was only taken seriously because it appeared to offer a solution to the inflationary problems of the period. MSV is the corporate version of neoliberal economic philosophy.

Berle and Means (1932) argued that the powers granted to a corporation or its management should be used exclusively for the benefits of shareholders. Jensen and Meckling (1976) developed this further stating that of all stakeholders in a company, shareholders face the greatest risk of receiving no returns on their contributions to the firm should it go bust. Therefore, they reasoned as the bearers of the greatest risk only shareholders should be entitled to profits if and when they materialise.

According to MSV the sole and only purpose of a company is to deliver and enhance the value of shareholders' investments and the company strategy should always be to try achieve a higher share price in order to maximise the returns for shareholders. On one level, this is a perfectly rational and understandable because when a company's share price rises and the company makes profits, then everyone benefits, including the workforce through their wages. As they pay taxes society also benefits. The profitable company also pays corporation tax, VAT and, where appropriate, business rates on the property it owns. Dividend payments made to shareholders are also subject to taxation.

A major issue about the relationship between the owners (shareholders) and the executive management of the company is how to ensure that the latter have the same motivation as the former. Jensen and Meckling (1976) argued that offering CEOs and the other company leaders financial incentives such as stock options and shares to "align their interest with maximising the stock price" would overcome the motivational problem of company management. This became a reality in 1993 when shareholders and management at last shared the same objectives.

According to Stout (2014) in a move that transformed the corporate outlook the US government requested public companies to base the pay of top executives on so-called objective performance metrics to qualify for full-time tax deductibility. The metric chosen to judge their performance was not only the salary of a CEO but also their shareholding in the company.

Linking the CEO salary with shares effectively transformed their relationship from being an agent to an active shareholder so maximising the company share price was now in their personal interests. One consequence of this has been the growth of public company executive pay which has created antagonism and division when others have been asked to restrict their wage growth. The pay level of public company CEOs has risen to many multiples in excess of average workforce pay. In the US and UK, the differentials of pay between the CEO and ordinary workers remains high. In 2024 according to the UK High Pay Centre, FTSE 100 chief executives were paid over 120 times the median UK full-time worker. CEO's were paid on average £4.7 million, the average salary of full-time UK workers in 2024 according to the Office of National Statistics was £35,880. The wider economic impact of making the company management shareholders is that it has encouraged them to pursue strategies that benefit the shareholders and their own pockets, driving companies for short-term profit gain.

Whether it meant to or not, one consequence of MSV was that public companies effectively cut themselves off from other stakeholders, including the communities in which they operate. Businesses, according to this rationale, should never become involved with society. The theoretical justification for this was provided by economists such as Milton Friedman, illustrated by his famous quote in 1962:

> There is only one social responsibility of business – to use its resources and engage in activities designed to increase its profits so long as it stays within the rules of the game, which is to say engages in open and free competition without deception or fraud.

For many this has become the clearest expression of MSV. However, Stout (2014) argues that MSV is based on fundamental misunderstandings of corporate law. Furthermore, argues Stout, MSV is promoted by financial economists such as Friedman for ideological reasons and pursued by public company management for their own financial benefit. MSV draws its strength from the belief that corporate law requires directors to maximise shareholder value and that company directors can be sued if they do not do this.

"The fatal flaw (of this argument) is that it fails to appreciate what corporations really are…" According to MSV corporations are owned by their shareholders. "Shareholders are the principals and directors' are the agents of the shareholders' agents…" (Stout, 2014)

Stout argues that legally, 'Corporations own themselves' or have no owners at all. The shareholders have, "a contract between the human shareholders and the corporate entity…" in much the same way for example that an employee has an employment contract with a company. Consequently, Stout (2012: 368) states that, "Corporate directors have no obligation to fulfil shareholders' requests because directors are not agents but rather fiduciaries for both the corporate entity and its shareholders."

For its numerous critics MSV has had a corrosive and destructive influence on society, the economy and been of poor value to those it purports to support, the shareholder. Clarke (2013) characterises MSV as one of the most 'destabilising ideologies' of modern times: "It has damaged and shrunk corporations, distracted and weakened managers, diverted and undermined economies and, most paradoxically, undermined the long-term interests of shareholders."

Locke and Spender (2011) argue that after 1980 public companies, "increasingly lived under the tyranny of stock valuation and the demands of institutional investors." To satisfy their demands, "corporate management tended to the bottom line, that is, shored up short-term profits….and its company's share price benefit accordingly."

Clarke (2013) believes that,

> During the later decades of C.20th the Anglo- American corporation was crudely transformed from being a wealth-creating vehicle for the wider community of stakeholders and whole economy into a bundle of assets with the sole purpose of benefitting shareholder interests.

An example of this is the huge amount of money wasted when companies use profits to buy shares back from shareholders. Share buy-backs from companies from existing shareholders is a controversial use of corporate profits. The rationale is that it enhances shareholder value – existing shareholders get the market value plus a premium for their shares – and it also helps raise the overall share price because a market has been provided for the shares. Clarke (2013), however, argues that they serve no useful purpose and do not strengthen the company's long-term future through, for example, investing in new capital equipment. Rather, share buy-back schemes "enrich executives who hold share options."

MSV has been the background to a series of corporate scandals such as Enron/Worldcom in the United States. The harshness of MSV and its contribution to widening social and economic gaps has encouraged alternative theories to develop in response to changing economic circumstances.

Efficient market hypothesis

Supporters of various social, economic and political theories sometimes present them as being as immutable, unchanging laws of nature and nowhere is this better illustrated than in the belief of the supporters in market forces. Theories develop and are sustained in specific and economic and political circumstances and the Efficient Market Hypothesis (EFM) can be regarded as another version to maintain market hegemony.

Many of its proponents argue that EMH is a successor to MSV (Laskin, 2010) and as it is driven by 'the market' has to be better than any alternative. The efficient market hypothesis argues that stock markets are 'fundamentally value efficient' and that a company's share price incorporates all the relevant information about its value, and the share price reflects the best possible rational estimate of the stock's likely future risks and returns. The market then sets the valuation of the company's share price.

According to Fama, who developed EMH (1965, 1978), market efficiency has three levels: weak, semi-strong and strong. In the weak version, market participants (that is the buyers and sellers of shares) do not have all the relevant information about a company. There are some however who do have more information about the company and they will perform better than those without it. Those with the information will be close to or inside the company and include not only company personnel, but also external consultants, such as accountants, PR consultants, lawyers, stockbrokers and merchant bankers.

In the medium version of the theory, everyone can access all relevant information about the company and this is reflected in the share price. The same insiders listed above, however, may still have access to non-public information and use this to their benefit, therefore again beating the market.

Finally, the EFM strong version argues that since all relevant information is reflected in the share price, no-one investor has an advantage over others because everyone has the same knowledge and understanding about the company. This however, must be an artificial situation and might occur when the company has an announcement to make. Papers on how the media influences share buying demonstrate that buying and selling activity increases when there is news about a company in the media.

Malkiel argues that it is (2000: 59)

> generally believed that securities markets are extremely efficient in reflecting information about individual stocks so that when information arises, the news spreads very quickly and is incorporated into the prices of securities without delay. Markets are amazingly successful devices for reflecting new information rapidly and, for the most part, accurately. Above all, we believe that financial markets are efficient because they don't allow investors to earn above average risk adjusted returns.

Yet what 'drives' the market are not abstract, mysterious powers, but specific actions carried out by companies deliberately designed to increase the share prices. External economic and political circumstances over which few have any control also affect the share price.

Supporters of EMH argue that as the market is driving the share price then it must be efficient because the market cannot be any other than efficient. EMH adherents are market fundamentalists believing that because the theory is 'market driven' then it must be more true and effective than other theories. Such fetishisation of the market and market forces is, however, far from being non-ideological as its supporters claim as it helps to embed the belief about the superiority of market forces in popular consciousness. Kay Review (2012: 41) commented on the "almost magical powers" attributed to 'the market' by some supporters of the theory:

> Anthropormorphisation of 'the market' in phrases such as 'markets think' or 'the view of the market' is common usage. It should hardly need saying that the market does not think, and that what is described as the view of 'the market' is simply some average of the views of market participants. 'The market' knows nothing except what the market participants know, although it is of course possible that the average of a range of competing views may be a better estimate of fundamental value than the opinion of some (or conceivably all) individual market participants. The assessment of 'the market' is therefore only as good as the quality of the analysis done by asset managers and those who advise asset managers.

There are also accusations that the Efficient Market Hypothesis has contributed to bad macro-economic policy making decisions because of its oversimplified belief in the market. Kay Review (2012: 41) also believes that too much information can create problems for investors:

> Bad policy and bad decisions often have their origins in bad ideas. We question the exaggerated faith, which market commentators place in the efficient market hypothesis, arguing that the theory represents a poor basis for either regulation or investment. Regulatory philosophy influenced by

the efficient market hypothesis has placed undue reliance on information disclosure as a response to divergences in knowledge and incentives across the equity investment chain. This approach has led to the provision of large quantities of data, much of which is of little value to the users. Such copious data provision may drive damaging short-term decisions by investors, aggravated by well-documented cognitive biases such as excessive optimism, loss aversion and anchoring.

Kay (2012) argues that the Efficient Market Hypothesis represents an idealised and simplified view about how modern markets operate and the modern shareholder has changed and is now characterised by what he calls asset managers or 'specialist' investment intermediaries.

As the retail investor has declined, along with pension funds, and insurers have reduced their investment in equities, these have been replaced by investors, some of whom are interested in long-term investments but many others are there to trade in shares.

Lynn Stout, the trenchant critic of the Shareholder Value Theory is also critical of the Efficient Market Hypothesis. As with Kay her criticism is that the model does not relate to the modern market.

It is nearly impossible today to find a finance economist under the age of fifty who would claim the stock market prices *always* capture true value.... But, substantial support remains for the claim that – barring unusual circumstances and occasional fits of collective investor irrationality – over the long-run, stock prices tend to be reasonably related to actual values.

(Stout, 2012: 64)

We see this market fetishisation at play every day in for example, everyday discourse about the economy in phrases such as, 'the market knows best' and 'the market cannot be bucked.' It suggests implicitly that there is no economic alternative to a market-based economy and has enabled politicians and media supporters argue that there can never be an alternative.

From the PR perspective Hoffman et al. (2018: 298) raise a simple but critical question: if all the information is clearly and equally available to everyone, why then do companies need IR companies?

From an economic perspective, it is far from self-evident why corporations should employ professionals to repackage, exclaim and contextualise information for the financial community.

Neither MSV nor EFM do anything to address the dislocation between society and company with the separation between society and business arguably becoming more pronounced. Alternative philosophies have emerged to re-place the economic harshness and the resulting social dislocation of EFM and MSV that attempts to meet society's changing needs.

Stakeholder theory

Critics of capitalism range from Marxists who envisage capitalism's inevitable replacement by a totally different social and economic order to those who believe in capitalism but want to moderate its harsher effects and work within the system to change it. Stakeholder theory developed as a direct rebuttal of the shareholder value theory and contrasts for example with Friedman's argument that businesses has no duty to become involved with society and its sole responsibility must be to their shareholders.

Stakeholder theory argues that shareholders are not the main 'owners' of the company and to operate effectively the company needs the participation and involvement of all stakeholders. Workers, suppliers, customers, the local community all have a 'stake' in the company. Freeman (1984) argues that stakeholder theory is better for business, and a company that effectively manages its stakeholder connections will survive longer and perform better.

> Shareholder value theory argues that shareholders, or owners are entitled to the residual gains that accrue from value creation and trade. Stakeholder theory suggests that matters are more complicated, that is, that stakeholder relationships are involved, and that human beings are more complex than the standard account assumes...

Commenting on stakeholder theory has become a huge industry with an estimated 36,000 articles and books about it. Critics of it argue this illustrates one of its problems: the theory may sound fine but there are few examples of where it works in practice or where it has significantly changed the culture and the operation of a company. For all the interest in it, Stakeholder Theory remains on the fringes of managerial theory (Key, 1999).

Critics such as Key argue that Stakeholder Theory lacks specificity and cannot be operationalised in way that allows for a scientific or objective inspection of its impact. Other critics argue that it is vacuous and an unrealistic picture of how a company operates. The theory assumes that a company can only be considered when it delivers value to the majority of its shareholders. Yet with different values and demands, the question is can there realistically be one measure of success relevant and appropriate to everyone?

Economic and environmental circumstances especially are forcing companies to change and there are encouraging signs that some CEOs understand that the dislocation between corporate activities and the impact on society cannot be sustained and is also bad for business. There is a growing acceptance that the pendulum has swung too far in one direction and that with the world facing issues such as environmental problems, businesses can no longer remain aloof from the rest of society.

In practice Stakeholder Theory manifests itself through Corporate Social Responsibility programmes which covers a range of activities ranging from charitable donations and using recycled paper in the company to encouraging staff to become involved in their local communities through clean-up campaigns or fund-raising for local charities. The benefits of CSR according to its proponents are that it impacts on two key stakeholders: employees and the community in which the company operates and providing a better and positive image of the company. However, Friedman (1962) argues that such community-based activities should not be regarded as acts of corporate social responsibility. "It may be in the long-run interests of a corporation that it is a major employer in a small community to devote resources to providing amenities to that community or to improving its government" but that such activities are not 'social responsibility' because, "they (the actions) are entirely justified in its (the corporation's) self-interest" (Friedman, 1962: 132).

One problem for proponents of Stakeholder Theory is proving to companies that the process goes beyond making the company and its employees feel good about themselves; supporters of stakeholder theory believe carrying out these socially responsible or charitable actions also makes a difference to a company's profitability. While there are many companies that not only allow but encourage corporate social responsibility programmes such as community clean-up projects that cost little or nothing to the company, however, the challenge for stakeholder theory is to prove that such activities not only do not have a financial cost but by engaging in them they benefit the company financially. The emergence of theories like Triple Bottom Line (TBL) can be seen as an attempt to prove this and encourage more businesses to be more environmentally active.

Triple Bottom Line

TBL is an attempt to put a financial value on the contribution of three different aspects of a business and is regarded as a practical application of Stakeholder Theory.

While essentially an accounting framework, TBL argues that companies should try and value their social and environmental performances, in the same way a monetary value is put on its corporate performance. According to TBL, corporate performance should be measured by three equal elements: profit, people and planet, it aims to measure the financial, social and environmental performances of a company over time rather than concentrate on a short-term framework. Unlike the current conventional focus on profits, a company that uses TBL considers the full and real cost of doing business including the environmental costs.

TBL originated with John Elkington (1994) and is another response to the role business plays in response to environmental issues. Elkington argued that TBL represented a direct challenge to company boards.

> Instead of just focusing on such issues such as the pay packets of 'fat cat' directors, new questions are being asked. For example, what is business for? Who should have a say in how companies are run? What is the appropriate balance between shareholders and other stakeholders? And what balance should be struck at the level of the triple bottom line? The better the system of corporate governance, the greater the chance that we can build towards genuinely sustainable capitalism.

Elkington (1994) argued that a fuller and fairer picture about a company's performance would result from having three, separate 'bottom lines' on the profit and lost account.

1 Traditional measure of corporate profit – bottom line of profit and loss account
2 People's account – a measure of how socially responsible a company has been through its operations. Companies must pursue objectives that are not simply economically justified but that are also ecologically and socially acceptable. This involves having a clear vision of a company and the needs and expectations of all stakeholders
3 The planet account – a measure of how environmentally responsible the company has been.

However, there are practical issues obstructing this, it is for example, difficult to measure the people and planet accounts in the same cash terms as profit.

TBL is perhaps the best known of several theories which emerged out of the growing awareness of environmental issues and the dissatisfaction with the social impact of MSV. All the theories were attempts to try to move the focus of a company away from financial performance being the main indicator of its performance. Other examples include the balanced scorecard (Kaplan and Norton, 1992), intellectual capital assessment, and environmental and social audits. These are all attempts to get a company to move beyond the limited focus on profits.

It does appear though that TBL is gaining traction in some quarters. According to Sridhar and Jones (2013), "Corporations are vigorously creating and publishing TBL reports in order to showcase an image of care for the economic, environmental and social dimensions of social responsibility."

A number of surveys appear to confirm that there is a growing business awareness about the importance of environmental issues among CEOs. The

2019 Deloitte Global Societal Impact Survey, 'The rise of the socially responsible business,' reported that 93% of business leaders believe companies are more than just employers: they are also 'stewards' of society. 95% of CEOs stated they were planning to take a bigger stance on societal impact issues.

Research by Ernst and Young (2023) demonstrates that many CEOs believe ESG is, above all, a major commercial and growth opportunity. 86% of CEOs say, "a focus on ESG and sustainable, inclusive growth have been critical to building trust with their stakeholders in today's uncertain times."

However, there is a large gap between recognising the importance of the issue and taking concrete steps to resolve the problem. Just how far is this issue integrated into corporate strategy and in what ways are actual business practices changing?

While these are all fine sounding statements many believe that in the current crisis we cannot rely on businesses to take action alone, and the only way real change will take place is through governments imposing change.

The sustainability and Environmental Social and Governmental agenda (ESG) is the link between business concerns and wider social and environmental issues. The Ernst and Young report (2023) provides a further indication of the way some businesses are changing.

> We are at a turning point in the sustainability and environmental, social governance (ESG) agenda. From within the organisation, executives are passionate about making a difference to the planet as well as building their companies resilience and long-term value. From the outside-in we have reached the point where investors, employees, consumers and the wider public simply expect a company to be addressing ESG priorities and opportunities. The sustainability agenda is redefining the relationship between European companies and their employees.

Enlightened shareholder value theory (ESV)

There have been several variations and attempts to develop the basic theories as a reaction to changing economic circumstances. Enlightened Shareholder Value, which is enshrined in company law in the UK through the 2006 Companies Act (specifically two parts SS 172 (1) and section 417 of the Act) argues that,

> The former lays down a duty for directors, namely they must do what they consider, in good faith will promote the success of the company for the benefit of the members. ESV affirms that the ultimate goal of the company is to benefit the members of the company but provides that in achieving this goal the directors must consider wider interests, such as the long-term effect of their decisions and the interests of other stakeholders such as employees.

This approach, while clearly based on shareholder value, excludes, "exclusive focus on the short-term financial bottom line and seeks a more inclusive approach that values the building of long-term relationships."

However, while Section 6 of the 2006 Act contains many worthwhile sentiments and statements about stakeholders, the reality is that they have no hold over the directors. They cannot, for instance, compel directors to take their interests into account.

"ESV codifies a restrained brand of shareholder value that provides that the stakeholders' interests need to be considered and there should not necessarily be an emphasis on short-term earning." According to the Quoted Companies Alliance, few of its member companies have noted any real impact.

6 Critical financial PR

A new paradigm for new times?

A new paradigm emerges out of debate and challenges to the existing paradigm and this book is a contribution to that debate. It argues that if financial communications is to contribute positively to a debate then it needs a new paradigm. It is not the purpose of this chapter to describe in detail what it might look like; instead its purpose is to outline some key themes it should have. Kersten (1994: 129) argues:

> PR like any other organizational activity is determined by its economic, political and ideological context. As long as there no significant changes in this context and in the relationship of PR to this context, it will be very difficult to create or even conceive of any meaningful changes in the practice of PR.

Ideology is all-pervasive and at its most dominating and distorting when we uncritically accept it in our everyday routine and social life. As we have seen, this is the current situation with market-based philosophy. The first step to change and develop an alternative, is a critical awareness. "For the PR field this means a recognition of the power relations in the organisation and an acknowledgement of its own ideological role in this acceptance." (Kersten, 1994)

Arguably a change is needed similar to the scale that emerged after the Second World War, when society by and large pulled together to re-build shattered economies, needs to develop to confront the profound challenges posed by issues such as global warming. Currently no such consensus exists with many major, influential companies and investors refusing to accept that the problem exists.

The starting point for new paradigm should be based in Critical PR.

DOI: 10.4324/9780429323584-6

Background of critical PR

Critical PR emerged as a response to Excellence Theory. Pieczka (2006) describes the 'excellence' paradigm as being 'not just a tentative proposition, but a whole way of thinking' that is systems-based, US-centric, and focused around functional job roles and quantitative research (L'Etang, 2008; Macnamara, 2012). Holtzhausen (2000) and McKie and Munshi (2007) move away from what they see as a narrow organisational-focused approach, towards a broader view of public relations as a change agent in community and political activism.

Sriramesh (2009) speaks of the need in PR scholarship to distance itself from its ethnocentric (one-approach-fits-all) approach, pointing out that much of the literature, including that surrounding 'excellence,' 'assumes a pluralistic democratic system as the environment where PR is most advanced and practiced in a strategic manner.'

Excellence Theory's lack of attention to power dynamics has also been highlighted (Coombs and Holladay, 2014). Dozier and Lauzen (2000) argue that the model does not address 'powerless publics,' or 'irreconcilable differences' in situations where activist publics oppose the fundamental existence of an organisation and its behaviour, and so no mutually beneficial arrangement can be sought. Other critical scholars take sociological and cultural perspectives (Macnamara, 2012), considering how both culture and PR are shaped by each other, offering other perspectives apart from those seen as Western- and corporate-dominated (Curtin and Gaither, 2005).

However, one criticism of critical PR is that it has not been used itself in practice.

Critical financial PR

It is not the intention here to provide a detailed description of what such a new paradigm might look like but to outline key elements that could contribute to it.

- Accept that market-based solutions cannot provide the answer to all economic and business problems
- Paradigm must include an environmental perspective
- Inclusive – should include all company stakeholders
- PR practitioners should begin to properly practice the boundary spanning role. Boundary personnel, public relations practitioners support organisational subsystems by helping them to communicate across the boundaries of the organisation to external publics and by helping them to communicate within the organisation.

Laskin of course claims that they do already operate in such a role, feeding back the views of shareholders to the company. In practice, they do not, because management do not want them to perform such a role. Besides it's not just the views of shareholders that needs to be considered but that of all stakeholders.

- Critical financial PR needs to be that and be prepared to say to executive management – 'you are wrong.'

Financial communications as mentioned above operates in a context and will only be able to develop an alternative when public companies seriously develop their own alternative paradigm. Currently the evidence for this seems doubtful.

Bibliography

Arfin, F.N. (1994) *Financial Public Relations*, Pitman Publishing, London.

Argawal, V., Taffler, R.J., Bellotti, X., and Nash, E.A. (2015) 'Investor Relations, Information Aysymmetry and Market Value', *Accounting and Business Research*, 46 (1), 31–50.

Arvidsson, S. (2012) 'The Corporate Communication Process between Listed Companies and Financial Analysts', *Corporate Communications*, 17 (2), 98–112.

Attard, B. (1994) 'The Jobbers of the London Stock Exchange an Oral History', *Oral History*, 22 (1), 43–48. JSTOR, http://www.jstor.org/stable/40179394 [accessed 19 April 2023].

Barber, B., and Odean, T. (2007) 'All that Glitters: The Effect of Attention and Newsrooms on the Buying Behaviour of Individual and Institutional Investors', *Review of Financial Studies*, 21, 777–818.

Barnes, B. (1982) *T.S. Kuhn and Social Science*, Red Globe Press, London.

Berle, A.A. and Means, G.C. (1932), *The Modern Corporation and Private Property*, New York, NY, McMillan

Bhattacharya, N., Galpin, N., Ray, R., and Yu, X. (2009) 'The Role of the Media in the Internet IPO Bubble', *Journal of Financial and Quantitative Analysis*, 44 (3) 657–682.

Black Rock. (2022) https://www.blackrock.com/corporate/newsroom/press-releases/article/corporate-one/press-releases/blackrock-creates-the-blackrock-foundation

Blackhurst, C. (2000) 'How the City Was Spun', *Management Today*, January/February, pp. 128–136

BNY Mellon, C. (2022) *The State of the US Retail Investor: Insights and Implications*, BNY Mellon, New York.

Boje, D.M. (2001) 'The Storytelling Organisation: A Study of Story Performance in an Office-Supply Firm', *Administrative Science Quarterly*, 36, 106–126.

Botan, C. (1993) 'Introduction to the Paradigm Struggle in PR', *Public Relations Review*, 192 (2), 107–110.

Botan, C.H. and Taylor, M. (2004), 'Public Relations State of the Field', *Journal of Communications*, 54 (4) (December, 2004) 645–661

Butterick, K. (2015) *Complacency and Collusion. A Critical Introduction to Business and Financial Journalism*, Pluto Press, London.

Campbell, G. Turner, J.D., Walker, C.B., (2012), 'The role of the media in a bubble', *Explorations in Media History*, 49, 461–481

Chapman, C. (2011) *Selling the Family Silver: Has Privatisation Worked?* Random House, London.

Clarke, T. (2013) 'Deconstructing the Mythology of Shareholder Value: A Comment on Lynn Stout's "The Shareholder Value Myth"', *Accounting Economics and Law: A Convivium*, 3 (1), 15–42.

Coombs, W.T. and Holladay, S.J. (2014) 'How publics react to crisis communication efforts: company crisis response reactions across sub-areas' *Journal of Communication Management*, 18 (1), 40–57

Curtin, P.H. (2012) 'Public Relations and Philosophy Parsing Paradigms', *Public Relations Inquiry*, 1 (1), 31–47

Curtin, P. and Geither, K. (2005), 'Privileging Identity, Difference and Power: The Circuit of Culture as a basis for Public Relations Theory' *Journal of Public Relations Research*, 17 91–95

Coyle, J. (2004) 'Flattery Will Get You Everywhere', *Observer*, 18 April, p. 13.

Daily Mail (1896) 'Advice to Investors', *Daily Mail Historical Archive*, 4 May, p. 2 [London, England] Web [accessed 14 November 2022]. www.gale.com/intl/c/daily-mail-historical-archive

Dale, R. (2004) *The First Crash: Lessons from the South Sea Bubble*, Princeton University Press, Princeton, NJ.

Davis, A. (2006) 'The Role of the Mass Media in Investor Relations', *Journal of Communication Management*, 10 (1), 7–17, Emerald Publishing.

Deloitte Global Societal Impact Survey (2019) 'The Rise of the Socially Responsible Business'.

De Santo, B., and Bradin, B. (2011) 'Financial Public Relations', in Moss, D., and De Santo, B. (eds), *Public Relations: A Managerial Perspective*, Sage, London. 243–264

Doan, M.A., and McKie, D. (2017) 'Financial Investigations: Auditing Research Accounts of Communication in Business, Investor Relations and Public Relations', *Public Relations Review*, 43, 306–313.

Dolphin, R.R. (2004) 'The Strategic Role of Investor Relations', *Corporate Communications*, 9 (1), 25–41.

Dougal, C., Engelberg, J., Garcia, D., and Parsons, C.A. (2012) 'Journalists and the Stock Market', *Review of Financial Studies*, 25 (3) 640–672, Oxford University Press.

Dozier, D.M., and Lauzen, M.M. (2000) 'Liberating the Intellectual from the Practice: Public Relations, activism and the role of the scholar, *Journal of Public Relations Research*, 12 (1) 3–22

Duguid, C. (1902) *How to Read the Money Article*, E. Wilson, London.

Dyck, A., Lins, K.V., Lukas, R., and Wagner, H.F. (2019) 'Do Institutional Investors Drive Corporate Social Responsibility? International Evidence', *Journal of Financial Economics*, 131, 693–714.

Ernst and Young (2022) 'How Can Boards Strengthen Governance to Accelerate Their ESG Journeys'.

Edwards, L., and Hodges, C.E., eds (2011) *Public Relations, Society and Culture*, Routledge, London and New York.

Elkington, J. (1994) 'Towards the Sustainable Corporation: Win-win Business Strategies for Sustainable Development', *California Management Review*, 36 (2), 90–100.

Engellberg, J.E., and Parsons, L.A. (2011) 'The Causal Impact of Media in Financial Markets', *The Journal of Finance*, 66 (1), 69–97.

Environmental Social and Governmental Agenda (ESG). EU. 2022

Fama, E.F. (1965) 'The Behaviour of Stock Market Prices', *The Journal of Business*, 38 (1), 34–105.

Fama, E.F. (1978) 'Efficient Capital Markets: A Review of Theory and Empirical Work', *The Journal of Finance*, 25 (2), 338–417.

Farraghe, E.J., Kleiman, R., and Bazaz, M.S. (1994) 'Do Investor Relations Make a Difference?', *The Quarterly Review of Economics and Finance*, 34 (4), 403–412.

Freeman, R.E. (1984) *Strategic Management: A Stakeholder Approach*, Pitman, Boston, MA.

Friedman, M. (1962) *Capitalism and Freedom*, University of Chicago Press, Chicago, IL.

Galbraith, J.K. (1993) *A Short History of Financial Euphoria*, Penguin, London.

Grunig, J., and Hunt, T. (1984) *Managing Public Relations*, Holt, Rinehart & Winston, New York.

Grunig, J.E. (2009) 'Paradigms of Public Relations in an Age of Digitalization', *PRism*, Jan, 6 (2) 1–9.

Gurrola-Perez, P., Lin, K., and Speth, B. (2002) 'Retail Trading an Analysis of Global Trends and Drivers', www.Worldexchanges/org/storage/app/media

Hayagreeva, R., and Sivakumar, K. (1999) 'Institutional Sources of Boundary-Spanning Structures: The Establishment of Investor Relations Departments in the Fortune 500 Industrials', *Organisational Science*, 10 (1), 27–42.

Holtzhausen, D.R. (2000), 'Postmodern Values in Public Relations, *Journal of Public Relations Research*' 12 (1) 93–114

Hoffmann, C.P., Tietz, S., and Hammann, K. (2018) 'Investor Relations – A Systematic Literature Review', *Corporate Communications: An International Journal*, 23 (3), 294–311.

Huang, Y.-H.C., and Lu, J.C. (2012) 'The Influence of Excellence: A Citation Analysis of Excellence Study in PR Scholarship, 1992–2011', in *Public Relations and Communications Management. The State of the Profession*. Proceedings of the 19th International PR Research Symposium, Bledcom. Bled, Slovenia

Hutton, W. (1995) *The State We're In*, Jonathan Cape, London.

Jameson, D.A. (2009) 'Economic Crises and Financial Disasters, the Role of Business Communication', *Journal of Business Communication*, 48, 499–504

Jeffries, L. (2010) *Critical Stylistics: The Power of English*, Palgrave Macmillan, Basingstoke.

Jensen, J., and Meckling, W. (1976) 'Theory of the Firm: Managerial Behaviour, Agency Costs and Ownership Structure', *Journal of Financial Economics*, 3 (4), 305–360.

Jeremy, D.J. (1998) *A Business History of Britain*, Oxford UP, Oxford.

Johnson-Young, E. and Magee, R.G. (2019) 'The CSR paradox, when a social responsibility campaign can tarnish a brand', *Corporate Communications, An International Journal*, 24 (1) 179–196

Kaplan, R.S., and Norton, D.P. (1992) 'The Balanced Scorecard: Measures that Drive Performance', *Harvard Business Review*, January–February, 70 (1), 71–79.

Kay Review (2012) *Kay Review of Equity Markets and Long Term Decision Making*, Department of Business Innovation and Skills, London.

Kelly, S.K., Laskin, V.A., and Rosenstein, G.A. (2010) 'Investor Relations: Two-Way Symmetrical Practice', *Journal of Public Relations Research*, 22 (2), 182–208, Taylor and Francis.

Kersten, A. (1994) 'The Ethics and Ideology of Public Relation: A Critical Examination of American Theory and Practice', in *Normative Aspekte der Public Relations*, Ambrecht, W and Zabel, U. (eds) , Westdeutscher Verlag. Opladen

Key, S. (1999) 'Towards a New Theory of the Firm: A Critique of Stakeholder Theory', *Management Decision*, 37 (4), 317–328.

Keynes, J.M. (1936) *The General Theory of Employment, Interest and Money*, Palgrave Macmillan, London.

Kindleberger, C.P., and Aliber, R.Z. (2005) *Manias, Panics and Crashes, a History of Financial Crises*, Palgrave Macmillan, London.

Kuhn, T. (1962) *Structure of Scientific Revolutions*, University of Chicago Press, Chicago.

Kynaston, D. (1994) *The City of London, Volume 1: A World of Its Own 1815–1890*, Pimlico, London.

Kynaston, D. (1998) *The Financial Times: A Centenary History*, Viking, London.

Laskin, A. (2010) *Managing Investor Relations: Strategies for Effective Communication*, Business Expert Press, New York.

Laskin, A., ed. (2018) *The Handbook of Financial Communications & Investor Relations*, Wiley and Blackwell, London.

Lee, M. (2014) 'A Review of Communication Scholarship on the Financial Markets and the Financial Media', *International Journal of Communications*, 8, 715–716.

L'Etang, J. (2008) *Public Relations, Concepts, Practice and Critique*, SAGE Publications, London

Li, Y. (2021) 'Gamestop, Reddit and RobinHood: A Full Recap of the Historic Retail Trading Mania on Wall Street', *CNBC.com* [accessed 30 January 2021].

Locke, R., and Spender, J.C. (2011) *Confronting Managerialism: How Business Elites Threw Our Lives Out of Balance*, Zed Books, London.

Logan, N. (2014) 'Corporate Voice and Ideology: An Alternate Approach to Understanding Public Relations History', *Public Relations Review*, 40, 661–668.

McKie, D. and Munshi, D. (2007) *Reconfiguring Public Relations, Ecology, Equity and Enterprise*, Routledge, London

Macey, J.R. and Miller, G.P. (1993) 'Corporate Stakeholders: A Contractual Perspective' *University of Toronto Law Journal*, 43, 401–424

Macnamara, J. (2012) *Organizational Listening: The Missing Essential in Public Communication*, Peter Lang Inc, Oxford.

Malkiel, B.G. (2000) 'The Efficient Market Theory and Its Critics', *Journal of Economic Perspectives*, 17 (1), 59–82.

Malkiel, B.G. (2003) 'The Efficient Market Hypothesis and Its Critics', *The Journal of Economic Perspectives*, 17 (1), Winter, 59–82.

Maltby, J. (1998) 'UK Joint Stock Companies Legislation 1844–1900: Accounting Publicity and "Mercantile Caution"', *Accounting History*, 3 (1), 9–32.

Marston, C. (1996) 'The Organisation of the Investor Relations Function by Large UK Quoted Companies', *Omega*, 24 (4), 47–88.

Marston, C., and Straker, M. (2001) 'Investor Relations: A European Survey', *Corporate Communications*, 6 (2), 82–93.

Martin, R., Casson, C., and Tahir, M.N. (2007) *Investor Engagement: Investors and Management Practice Under Shareholder Value*, OUP, Oxford.

McCusker, J.J. (1991) 'The Demise of Distance: The Business Press and the Origins of the Information Revolution in the Early Modern Atlantic World', *The American Historical Review*, 110 (2), 1–28.

McLellan, D. (1986) *Ideology*, University of Minnesota Press, Minneapolis.

Moloney, K. (2006) *Rethinking Public Relations: PR, Propaganda and Democracy*, Routledge, London.

Parsons, W. (1989) *The Power of the Financial Press*, Edward Elgar, London.

Pieczka, M, (2006) 'Paradigms, Systems Theory and Public Relations' in *Public Relations: Critical Debates and Contemporary Practice*, L'Etang, J. and Pieczka, M. (eds), Lawrence Erlbaum Associates, Mahwah, NJ

Poovey, M. (2002) 'Writing About Finance in Victorian England: Disclosure and Secrecy in the Culture of Investment', *Victorian Studies*, 45, 17–21.

Porter, D. (1998) 'City Editors and the Modern Investing Public: Establishing the Integrity of the New Financial Journalism in Late Nineteenth Century London', *Media History*, 4 (1), 49–60.

Porter, D. (2004) 'Alsager, Thomas Masa (1779–1846)', in *Oxford Dictionary of National Biography*, Oxford University Press, www.oxforddnb.com/view/article/41071 [accessed 19 September 2021].

Preda, A. (2009) *Framing Finance: The Boundaries of Markets and Modern Capitalism*, University of Chicago Press, Chicago, IL.

Pratley, N. (2003) 'Digital Shareholders Could Recreate some of the buzz we lost', *The Guardian* 14th April, 32

Pugh, P. (1998) *The Strength to Change: Transforming a Business for the 21st Century*, Penguin Books, London.

Richardson, J.E. (2007) *Analysing Newspapers: An approach from Critical Discourse Analysis*, Palgrave Macmillan, Basingstoke

Robb, G. (2002) *White Collar Crime in Modern Britain: Financial Fraud and Business Mortality 1845–1929*, Cambridge University Press, Cambridge.

Roush, C. (2006) *Profits and Losses: Business Journalism and Its Role in Society*, Marion Street Press, Oak Park, IL.

Schiller, R. (2000) *Irrational Exuberance*, Princeton University Press, Princeton, NJ.

Scott, W.R. (1951) *The Constitution and Finance of English, Scottish and Irish Joint Stock Companies to 1790*, 3 vols., Peter Smith, New York.

Sheridan, T., and Kendall, N. (1992) *Corporate Governance*, Financial Times Pitman Publishing, London.

Sridhar, K., and Jones, G. (2013) 'The Three Fundamental Criticisms of the Triple Bottom Line Approach: An Empirical Study to Link Sustainability Reports in Companies Based in the Asia-Pacific Region and TBL Shortcomings', *Asian Journal of Business Ethics*, 2, 91–111.

Sriramesh, K. (2009) 'Globalization and Public Relations' in *Public Relations Research: European and International Perspectives and Innovations*, Zerfass, A., Van Ruler, Sriramesh, K. (eds), VS Verlag Fur Sozialwissenschaften, Wiesbaden

Stout, L. (2012) *The Shareholder Value Myth: How Putting Shareholders First Harms Investors, Corporations and the Public*, Berrett-Koehler, San Francisco, CA.

Stout, L. (2014) 'The Corporation and the Law', *Proceedings of the American Philosophical Society*, 158 (4), December, 364–371.

Tambini, D. (2010) 'What Are Financial Journalists For?', *Journalism Studies*, 11 (2), 158–174.

Taylor, J. (2012) 'Watchdogs or Apologists? Financial Journalism and Company Fraud in Early Victorian Britain', *Historical Research*, 85 (230), November, 632–650.

Tetlock, P.C. (2007) 'Giving Content to Investor Sentiment: The Role of the Media in the Stock Market', *The Journal of Finance*, LXII (3), June, 1139–1167.

Tuominen, P.P. (1997) 'Investor Relations: A Nordic School Approach', *Corporate Communications*, 2 (1), 46–55.

Van Oss, S.F. (1898) 'The Limited Company Craze', *Nineteenth Century*, 43, 48–63.

www.fti.consulting.com [accessed 15 June 2022].

Printed in the United States
by Baker & Taylor Publisher Services